Would Anyone Cry For Me?

Thanks for your support!
Love,

Would Anyone Cry For Me?

A True Story For All Silent Hurting Hearts

Betty Thompson Haygood

Published By: Betty Thompson Haygood LLC

DEDICATION

To All victims who have suffered the hurt of your own Devil Man or Woman, I know your heart, and I feel your tears. I am you and you are me; together we can become the free hearts we all long to be.

In memory of my brother and sister, Asa Jerome Thompson, Sr. and Dale McLaughlin, and my mother-in-law, Ms. Mozell Broadway

ACKNOWLEDGMENTS

First, honor is due to God who wrote this book through me. I ran for ten years from writing, but He did not give up on me.
Life itself would not be possible for me without my two wonderful, supportive parents: Harry & Ella Mae Thompson. Thank you for loving me.
To my four sisters: Pat (Clarence), Gloria, Renda, and Wendy, and my brother: Harry (Ariska). "You all have helped to shape me into the person I am today."
To my son Vent Syrell (Angela), you have loved me through the early years of learning to be a mom, thanks for forgiving my shortcomings. To my two daughters, Taiasha and Shameka (Joshua). Where would a mom be without two wonderful daughters like you?
A special thank you to Lanita (Anthony), Sonya (Frank), Faye (Jack), Courtney, and Ennis Jr. Thanks for always loving me and giving me feedback.
A special thank you to those of you behind the scenes helping to make this book a reality: Jason (Terra) at Ayers Production, thanks for your production of our trailer; Tina (Preston) Parker, Meme (Stan) Birchfield, and Dr. Gwendolyne at Corrective Measures LLC. Thanks for editing, and proofing our book; and Don (Judy) Axsom, thank you for designing the cover of our book; Paul Trostle Jr., thanks for being my website IT Guy/Nephew; Vatrice (Michael) Lanier, at Lanier and Lanier, Thank you for helping to market our book.

To Isiah, my patient, loving, and dedicated husband: I am here at this stage in my life because of your allowing me to be myself. Always encouraging, always believing. I am blessed to be one with you.

Preface: My reality is that I have a husband who has changed the way I look at the world. He makes me so happy that I don't remember my sadness.

I remember when we first got married and he asked me, "What will you give and put into this marriage? What do you think marriage is made of?" I quickly responded, "50/50." To my dismay, his response was, "Then we are doomed to fail." He continued, "Unless you give 100% of you and I give 100% of me, we are destined not to last joyfully."

Quickly I found myself saying, "Let me ponder that." It took me days of praying and meditating to realize my husband was right. I had planned on giving a part of me but I wanted to reserve a little in case my world got shattered and the marriage didn't work. I never realized that if I reserved even 1% of my all, that I could possibly miss out on all life had to offer.

Then a light went off inside and I truly decided to give my marriage 100%, of me. There would be dedication, and oh, what a marriage God has blessed us with!

But as happy as my life is now, it wasn't always this way.

This true story will take you to the core of my living hell, the darkness of my childhood, and an adulthood that often left me crying for escape. I will share with you my terror of child abuse by a trusted grown neighbor, murder, onto free sex for all, to adultery, and finishing with a spin in the gay lifestyle. I was the worst and lowest of all mankind.

Because of mercy, grace and my willingness to change, I am a new me. A me that I love. A me that can look in the mirror and like the woman looking back. My biggest prayer is that this book will help the millions of you reading see that this can be your success story as well.

If you have ever felt like the dirt under other people's shoes, the ugliest of all creation, the addict, the killer, the helpless, the adulterous, the liar and, most of all, the one who can never be forgiven for the life you have led, know that you are not alone. I've been where you are. I know that no one has to stay in darkness, sadness, or bondage. A new life is just a decision away. Only you can make that decision for your life.

The light at the end of your tunnel can start shining today.

Know that this book is laying me bare and showing the world the truth of who I am and was. As I write, sometimes I cannot believe that it is I writing. I am compelled to think more about you and about this book helping you than about how I look as a person. My dirt can be your detergent. My sorrows can help you with your pains. My outcome can show you the way to your own joyful outcome. Look beyond the horrors, but remember that I am real. Look beyond the stories, but remember that they are genuine and true. Allow this book to help you look into yourself, to remember how you got to where you are. Know, without a shadow of a doubt, that you are special and that there is a special place of peace here on this earth just waiting for you.

CONTENTS

Disclaimer: *Please read before you venture into this book. Chapter One is a very graphic chapter about abuse and innocence lost. I wrote about these incidents in a way to help some readers to see the devastation of life and to help others remember their own devastation. In many cases, unless you see the events and the emotions behind them, you will not be able to see why a person's life turns out the way it does. With the victims of child abuse, it is sometimes hard to understand why they feel crazy in their hearts and in their minds. It is my hope that by your reading and understanding the events that happened to me (and so many of you), it will help you to comprehend what we, and so many others, have gone through. God placed this on my heart in these words so that healing can come for all. Please do not let Chapter One stop you from reading this book in its entirety. For as dark as the beginning is, you will see light at the end of my tunnel and, prayerfully, your own!*

You'll never find my story in a fairy tale; I once felt like no other woman in the world. My world was filled with shame, pain, darkness, sorrow, rejection, loneliness, and hurt. For most of my life, I thought I did not show it, but I acted it out. I fooled myself so much I did not recognize the woman in the mirror, nor did I like her. She was everything I did not want to be, but at that time, I did not know how to change.

One

Memories

How does one talk about their life? Make believe is easy… you just write down the fantasy of whom you want to be. Truth is different because it enters into a part of you that reaches to your core. It exposes the person you are deep down inside. There is only one person who truly knows, and that person is the one who stares back at you in the mirror. We can dress ourselves up and look like we have it all together, but when the music stops playing and we are alone with ourselves, who are we?

The first thing I remember from my youth is wanting to be a singer. I wanted to put a smile in people's hearts and on their faces through my music. I remember being in a dream – like trance and looking up into the sky. A lot of angels were there and they were talking. God told them, "Be quiet and listen to my child. See how beautiful her voice is." It was the happiest day I could remember. I knew that I had someone who believed in me and I believed in Him: "my God."

As quickly as the wind blows, the memory vanishes and a second enters my mind. If ever there were opposites, this would be it. It is a memory so horrible that I am almost not able to speak about it. It always brings tears to my eyes.

I was born in 1963 and raised in a family of seven children. I was number four. We were raised in the country and there were only a few neighbors. All of my neighbors were relatives except in one house next door. During the summer we would go out into the neighborhood and into the woods next to our home. We would play all day and even eat in the woods on berries and fruits. I remember climbing trees and thinking life could not be any better. In our childhood, we did not know anything about racism or being rich or poor. Our parents taught us that grown-ups are always right; and love and forgiveness are the keys to happiness and freedom. They taught us that God hears our prayers, and He always protects His children. I believed this with all my heart. When you hear my epic horror, you will know why my world and I were so shattered.

It was a normal sunny summer day. My siblings and I were headed for our cousin's house. All of the houses had a little distance between them. They were not like the houses of today, which are so close together you can hear your neighbors talking. I was not quite ready when everyone else was, so I told them I would catch up with them shortly. I finished getting dressed and headed to my cousin's house to play. I do not remember what my mom was doing or where she was. In those days, everyone trusted their neighbors. It was a time when neighbors protected each other. There was no need for her to make sure I got to my cousin's house safely. I did it all the time. I believe I was about 9 or 10 years old.

Only one house in the neighborhood could afford a telephone. It belonged to our next door neighbor. When I passed the neighbor's home, one of the grown sons (who was my parent's age) asked me to come in the house. Not sensing any cause for alarm, I said okay and went inside. When I got inside, Devil Man, – yes, Devil Man is the name I will give to the man with no heart or soul, – told me to go into his mother's room. I felt a little uneasy, but he was a grown-up and I knew I had to do what he told me. He asked me if I wanted to play with their telephone. If I wanted, I could lift it up off the receiver and hear the dial tone. For just a second I felt like he just wanted to play with me. I lifted up the telephone and heard the dial tone. It was a standard rotary phone, white in color. I remember how, when you dialed it, it went *click, click, click*. He allowed me to do this a few times until he could see some of the fear leave me. Then he told me I had to lie on the bed.

Devil Man was a tall man of nearly 6 feet. To me he was a giant. He had light skin and dark hair. I think he had on jeans and a shirt; but honestly, those things escape me. He had a girlfriend and he looked like a normal guy. He was polite to people. From the outside you would never know you were looking at pure evil. Sometimes, I wonder if he knew this about himself. Was he evil, or did he have a hard life, unseen by all? I distinctly remember his power and my weakness.

I could feel my little heart starting to race. Something in me knew danger was upon me. Why did I need to lie on the bed? What had I done? My words would not come out of my mouth because I was not allowed to talk back to grown-ups. I proceeded to do what he told me. I could not get on the bed by myself, so he lifted me. Inside I was screaming out, "Help! Someone please help me!" I prayed someone would come to rescue me, but no one came. I was under the control of Devil Man, the personal destroyer of my young world.

First, he took off my underwear and stood there looking down at me. He just stared. I remember looking at him for just a moment before looking away. I was so ashamed, so trapped, and so alone. He then lifted my dress up again and looked at me. He touched me with his hand. I think I started to cry a little because he gave me the hand part of the telephone to play with again. I clung to it as if it would save me from what was about to happen. He touched me again. This time between my legs and something strange happened. I felt a mixture of horror and a hint of pleasure. My mind was about to explode. I could not understand what I was feeling. This man was taking away all of my innocence and everything pure about me. For an instant, I thought his touch felt good. I did not know how to handle this feeling so I lay there in shock wondering what was going on. I was frozen, like a deer caught in headlights. I wanted to run but my body would not respond to my commands. The next thing I remember was him zipping down his pants. I thought, "Why is he doing that?"

Everything seemed to happen in slow motion. I felt like I had been lying there forever. He let first his pants fall down. He pulled his underwear down. He told me, "Touch this," while putting his male stick part in my little hands. He said, "Rub it for me," and I did. I didn't understand why he rolled his head back and groaned. As I rubbed, it seemed to grow and get bigger. This scared me; but at the same time it was unique in itself. I rubbed it for what seemed like forever before he touched me with it. First, he put it on my stomach; and then he ran it along my thigh. After that he opened my legs with his hands and told me not to make a sound. He ran that thing up my inner thigh and then he touched it. He touched the part of me that only a husband has permission to touch. He ran it up and down my girly part for a while. When he tried to penetrate, he was too big and it hurt. I started to cry. He bent down to lick me for a while. His tongue was so hot. Again, I had this feeling that what he was doing felt good, but how could it when he had no right to be doing it? He licked for a while longer before he inserted his tongue into the forbidden zone. I went into a state of shock. For some reason, I became wet. I think this is what he was trying to achieve because he stood up, took that male stick of his in his hand and put it on me again. He put it all over my girlie area and tried to enter me again. He kept trying when, all of a sudden, I heard him breath hard and a lot of this hot stuff came out on me. He stood there for a few minutes looking dazed and confused. Then he put on his shorts and pants. He looked down at me as if trying to decide what to do with me. I dared not move or speak. He put on my underwear, pulled down my dress, put me on the floor, and told me to go home. He told me if I told anyone what had just happened, they would tell me I was a bad girl and it was my fault. He said my parents would spank me, and no one would want to play with me or be my friend again.

When he opened the door to let me out of the prison I had been in, I ran straight home. My sunny joyful day had turned into dread. The sky didn't look as bright and the sun didn't feel as warm. When I walked into the house, one that used to be warm and inviting, I found it small and cold. The brown walls seemed a little bit duller and the floors seemed a little more torn and worn. The sadness in my heart overflowed into my every thought.

When I had walked out of this home, what seemed like hours ago, I had been a normal happy little girl. Now as I stepped back in, I was a stranger in my own skin. I was a mess. There was a stranger in the house. When I looked in the mirror, the stranger was me.

I felt like I had been split into two different people – the girl whom everyone saw and the bad girl who had been just created. If I ever thought I was pretty, I knew that I was pretty no more. If I ever thought I was special, I knew I was special no more. How do I explain who I now was? I had felt like I was a beautiful tree growing in a beautiful forest. My leaves were rich in color and my bark was strong. Then the forest fires in the form of Devil Man came to burn me to pieces. My leaves would no longer blow in the wind. My protective bark was black, sooty, and destroyed. I could not conceive, that somewhere in this dead tree, was a new branch with a few beautiful green leaves. That would have meant that somewhere there was life still in the tree/me.

The only one in the house was my mom. There was no way I could tell her. I could not tell her that everything good in me had just been ripped out. I could not tell her that I was scared and confused. I could not tell her that what was pure in me was pure no more. All I wanted to do was run into her arms for safety, but how could I when I felt that I had done such a bad and unforgivable thing? Instead, I went into the bedroom I shared with five of my siblings; I found a pair of dry underwear and proceeded to put them on. I took a towel and wiped myself off, although I did not believe I could wipe off the hurt and shame of what had just taken place. I remember twisting my panties up and hiding them in the trash can. I knew I could not explain to my mom how they had gotten so wet. As I hid the panties, I tried to hide my shame.

I stayed in the house the rest of that day, telling my mom that I did not feel well. I could not tell her my girlie part was on fire. The truth would create questions I had no answers for. Also I was fearful that telling the truth would cause me to be punished. I could not bear two punishments in one day, so I told her that my stomach hurt. I asked myself in silence, *"When will this pain go away?"* Then I answered, *"Never."*

When Mom was not around, I found myself crying. But why was I crying? Did I not bring this on myself the way Devil Man said I did? Was it not my fault he felt a need to touch me with himself? Did I not do something to bring all of this on my own head? I could not find any answers, so I started to pray about it.

I do not know how long I prayed. It could have been weeks or it could have been months or even years. All I know is that my prayer went like this: *"God, am I not your little girl? What did this man do to me? More than that, why did You let him? I thought You protected the ones You love. Do You not love me? I sing to You and pray to You all the time. What have I done wrong that You would allow Devil Man to hurt me like this? Can You please punish him so that he will not hurt me or anyone else ever, ever again, please?"*

Every day I prayed this prayer. One day someone came to our house and said Devil Man died while racing his car. This news should have made me happy. It did for an instant, but then everyone started to cry for this man. I began to feel guilty. I thought, "I prayed for him to be punished just like this and now I have killed him." I felt it was my fault. Inside, I was crying out for forgiveness; but on the outside no one knew my torment. Then other side of me came out. I said to myself, "Good for you, Devil Man. You got just what you gave me – pain. Try to hurt me now. Can you reach up from the pit of hell and hurt me? No, I do not think so. Your nasty hands will never touch me again. I will never be scared of you again. But in the place of you, your gift to me is that now I am afraid of all men. Will I never be free of this? How can I when no one can ever know what you did?"

I did not go to his funeral, nor did I want to. When my parents returned home from the funeral, I had an odd feeling. It felt like when they buried him, they had also buried a part of me. I should have felt free, but I felt like I was even more imprisoned. Now, he could never say those important words, "I am sorry for destroying you and your youth!"

I found myself praying a different prayer. My new prayer asked God for forgiveness – to forgive me for asking Him to protect me and for my causing this man his death. I bundled everything that had happened together and put it all on my plate. Like a criminal with a secret I wanted to free myself and tell, but the fear of punishment and desertion kept the words quiet and captive in my broken heart.

The Devil Man left me with something else though. It was

something unheard of. He left me wanting to feel a part of what he had made me feel on that day. I could not understand this. It was the worst day of my life yet, I longed to feel the sensation of what I had felt on that day. I wanted to cut my brain out and look at it to see why it was broken. Why did it, want this feeling? I thought, "Maybe Devil Man was not the sick one; maybe it was me." I found myself touching my private parts trying to get the same sensation. Sometimes, I could get some type of stimulation; but it was not the same. I wanted someone to give that feeling to me but I was scared. The fear of being hurt again as well as the anguish of thinking I had gone crazy haunted me. Surely only a demon-possessed child could have these thoughts. When I considered giving it any real thought, I trembled on the verge of tears. I did not think I could live through something like that happening to me again. The thoughts and manipulations bounced around in my mind for years. There was no healing because no one knew I was sick. I was always crying out for help, but no one could help me because I only cried out in my own mind.

The shame and despair of who I had become took me to a mighty dark place. There was no key to get out because I couldn't escape the prison of myself. Who would I become if I was to become anyone at all?

When I think back to those days, I still tremble. In the new me, I am convinced all darkness can turn into light. No one has to be a slave in their own body forever. However I am getting ahead of myself. "Rome was not built in a day," and neither was I.

Would Anyone Cry For Me?

Two

Walking The Wall

Truth be told, there is no perfect parent. We all make the most incredible mistakes, but the sad part about it is that at the time our children are growing up we think we know it all and know it best. It's usually not until our kids are grown up (and us too!) that we realize the many areas in which we could have done a better job in. Show me someone who thinks they know it all and I will show you a fool.

It is only when we open ourselves up to ask lots of questions and get lots of advice that we make wise decisions? The hard decisions like dealing with the unforgiveness of past hurts with our parents or rethinking the pain in our hearts that took years to make. Forgiveness is the powerful tool you do not always realize you have tucked away in your heart. The easiest way to forgive your parents is to look at your own life as an example and see how many bad decisions you have made. How many people have you hurt? How many times have you said to yourself, "I wish I could take that back?" Your reflection will show you that no one is perfect. No matter how many TV shows you watch that say otherwise, believe me when I say, no one!

My memories of my childhood and my parents are a big part of my life. How lonely I felt sometimes. It is a journey of how we all overcame the pain. Today we have the deepest love and respect for each other. It wasn't an overnight success. It took openness, crying, and honesty from all of us.

I did not realize it at first, but I became afraid of all men on the day I encountered Devil Man. I feared even the man who should be my protector, my dad. I found myself afraid to be alone in the room with him or any other man. No one knew this because I hid it by just making sure it never happened.

What do I remember most about the dad of my childhood? I used to call it "walking the wall." We grew up in a small country town called Hopkins. On the surface, everyone was polite and smiled. Looking back, I can now see the pressure of life everyone was going through. The men were hard workers. Most of us grew up in a two-parent home. Divorce was not a part of our environment and was not in our vocabulary.

But Fridays were different. That's when the weekend alcoholics would come out. They would start drinking after work on Friday and finish up on Saturday night,-using Sunday to start sobering up in order to be fit for work on Monday. This went on for many, many years; and it happens even today. My dad was no exception to this tradition. He would leave my mom and our family to go out with his friends (doing the kinds of things we all ask forgiveness for later.)

The pressure this must have put on my mom, raising seven kids, was amazing. We were all within 15 months of our next sibling. We laugh now that the only thing that truly sticks out most in our memories is getting what seemed like a daily spanking. When we confronted Mom as adults, she laughed and said, "I had to keep you all in control; otherwise, I would have run myself crazy trying to care for you." We laughed as well, remembering how mischievous we were. I see how difficult it is for parents raising one child: so someone please give my mom an award!

Daddy would party and spend the hard earned family money on his friends. He did not give it a second thought. His pleasure was the only thing that mattered. In the wee hours of the morning, he would drive up in the yard knowing that he had come to his safe place, home. With alcohol reeking on his breath, he always knew my mom would take care of him. He would stagger into the house and request food. My mom obliged him nearly every time. I could not understand at the time why she was so giving to him. In fact, I thought she was a weak woman. In time, I understood. She told us marriage is a commitment and not a convenience. God does not give you more than you can bear; and all things, even the things which seem unbearable, can one day

13

work out for the good. "Right," I said to myself.

My mom often said three words that have stayed with me. I even find myself saying them to my children: "Time will tell." These words freed me because they taught me that it does not matter what someone tells me because time will tell. Time exposes the good, the bad, and the ugly of their words. The one good thing this taught me was that you do not give up on your husband or friends when times are bad. You work through the problems toward good times.

My mom also taught us that it is easy to see the ugly in others; however if we try first to see the good in them, it opens the door for forgiveness. Our forgiveness frees our hearts to be able to go to a higher degree of loving others. Forgiving doesn't mean excusing bad behavior. My mom would say, "If you see the bad in someone, you have to know that there is something good in that person as well. Forgiving them keeps your heart healthy. It keeps you from becoming a bitter person. You don't take their actions against you so personally. You realize that person is sad somewhere in their heart. They may have low self-esteem or feel inadequate in life for all kinds of reasons. They may have gotten hurt and have never been able to get over it." She would continue, "It's a sad thing when a person has emptiness of heart. If we don't show them our love, our unconditional love, how else will they know the door to change is right around the corner for them?"

I remember one occasion when I could not sleep. I was still up when I saw the lights coming down around the corner of the dirt road we lived on. My dad was coming home. Something in me became scared. I ran off to bed, so he would not know I was awake. He came into the house. As my mom got up to take care of him, I listened. He requested food and, again, Mom fed him. After he finished, he laid his shoulder on the wall for support and walked the wall to bed. This went on for years. I could tell my mom was in constant prayer for my dad, her children, and her marriage.

Even the faithful have moments of weakness. One morning after my dad had stayed out all weekend, he tried to come in the door. We all knew something was wrong because my mom stood in the door when he arrived. When he requested to come in, my mom replied, "Not this morning." My dad reminded her it was his house. He paid the bills and made the rules for his house. Quickly, my mom pulled out a little gun my dad had purchased and repeated, "Not today." My dad, believing that my mom was kidding, decided to try and come in anyway. My mom shot a bullet in the ground and said again, "Not today!" Looking into my mom's dark brown eyes, my dad saw she was not kidding. For the first time, she had had her fill of his uncaring actions. He realized she was mind-blowingly furious and left to give her the time she needed to cool off. Little did we know that shortly after that incident, Dad took the gun and gave it away. Laughing, he told us 20 years later that he did not want Mom to change her mind and hit her target the next time.

Mom did cool off and things went back to what we called normal. Mom would pray and Daddy would play. What a pair! As I think about it now, they taught me the importance of not giving up when the going got rough. These lessons are close to my heart and helped to make me the person I now am. At the time, it hurt more than I thought we could bear. We had a dad that did not want to be with his family, a dad who thought everyone else's happiness meant more than the broken heart of his wife.

Then the unthinkable happened. I was about 12 or 13 at the time. I do not remember all the details, but my dad became very sick. He went to the dentist and had an abscess removed. He was okay the first day but became very sick and had to be hospitalized the next day. No matter what the physicians tried, he got worse and worse. Finally, they decided the only hope my dad had of surviving was to be transported to Charleston from the local hospital. My father was dying, and the staff knew it.

My dad had been in the local Columbia hospital for a long time. With the exception of only two friends, none of his running buddies did anything to help his family. They never even brought over a loaf of bread to feed his seven children. Every week my dad took his hard-earned money to spend on his friends; but when he could no longer supply them with fun, they were nowhere to be found. I am not sure how we survived, but God had mercy on us and we did. I don't ever remember being hungry, but I do remember always having just enough.

When I explained to my parents that God had selected me, His most ordinary daughter, to write a book, they were initially hesitant. I told them, "It will be a healing book about our family. We must all tell the highs and lows of where we've been," I said. I wanted to talk about Dad's dark days, with his permission, to help others.

My dad said, with the humblest of hearts, "You could fill your whole book with my life. I've come from a place where I know so many others want to come out of. I know that it was all for a time such as this."

The rest of my parent's story is this. Dad got worse. The hospital in Charleston was the last resort. My dad said he must have passed into the other world because he tells the following story about how he was saved and what changed his life.

"I remember seeing a light, and I knew it was the light of God coming to take my spirit. At that point, I knew I did not want to die because I knew what and who I was. I asked the Father to give me one more chance. I promised Him that I would become a husband to my wife and a father to my children. God said He would grant me time, and I have kept my promise ever since. I have changed my purpose in life and have decided that partying, playing, and alcohol would no longer be my pride and joy. I knew I no longer needed them to make me feel like a man. I had gotten approval from my Maker that my life means something. He sees me and that was all I needed all I ever needed. I was just looking in all the wrong places. The doctors saw life come back into my father's body and were amazed. They took him off all of the medicine, and he got well. Within a few weeks, he was able to come home. The true test of my dad's word to God would be shown for what it was.

One of the first noticeable things Dad did was to quit partying with his old crowd. He took my mom out dancing! He found joy in the wife of his youth. He loved being her husband. His view was still that men worked outside the house while women worked inside. Now, however, he was home to show my two brothers how it was done.

One day Dad came home and told Mom that with the seven children getting older, eating more, and needing more in supplies for school and afterschool activities, he needed to get a second job to support the family. Mom looked at him in a concerned way. She told him that if he got a second job, the family would never see him because he would always be working. She complimented him on the father and husband he had become and then said to him, "What do you think about my getting a job instead? This way we can spend time with the children after work every day. We can be a family. Harry, please let me to do this to help the family." Mom told Dad that since all the children were almost old enough to be in school, this could work out for the best for the family.

Daddy said, "Okay, but only if we can find someone we can trust to be home with the children while we are at work." My mom was overjoyed because she knew she would ask her mom to watch over us until we were in school. My mother explained to my grandmother the benefit of her working: she would get paid and my grandmother would get paid.

This extended family of caring and loving worked out

for everyone. With my grandmother keeping us, she was able to purchase her first home. We were taken care of by someone who really loved us.

When my mom went down to the unemployment office, they were testing girls to become seamstresses. My mom did not know a whole lot about sewing. She prayed she would know what to do and that she might get the job. The prayer was quickly answered. She did get the job and worked with the company over 20 years. She sure took good care of us along with my dad. The best part about this portion of our story is that I get to share how my mom's mother, our grandma, loved us so very much and took such wonderful care of us.

The second thing my dad did was to put the bottle down. He did this purely from his commitment to God. His faith in God's giving him a second chance gave him the strength he needed. I haven't seen my dad drunk since then. Society doesn't speak enough about the power of being resolved to change. My dad showed us that if you make up your mind, you can do anything.

He went to games at his children's high school. My dad enjoyed spending time with us. We went to parks to have picnics. He took us to the beach. He gained our love and our trust by his actions. We began to feel like our dad was our protector. He was always around to encourage us to be the best we could be. Here was a man with a sixth grade education who was taking care of our very large family.

My dad told me recently that one of his biggest regrets was not spending more time with us. He wished that he could have helped more to mold us into adults. Without hesitation, I reminded my dad of how much we all loved him and how we have all turned out okay. Through my mom and dad, we all know that we have hope!

Dad became active in church. He wanted other young men to know that the emptiness they felt was repairable. He urged them to not waste the many years with their families as he had done. Dad let them know that times were hard but they could be molded into being better men for their families. He taught them that they did not have to be what society says they are but could show society that all men are equal and want the same thing for their families.

Had I remembered this I would have saved myself from my greatest beating — and I do mean beating. I was to sing in the 1977/78 Miss Eagle Pageant at school. I needed the piano brought down from the music room to the cafeteria for the pageant. I went to Mr. Brown, a tall, thin, older black man who was a teacher at our school. He was known for always joking with the students. I asked him if he could help me find some guys who could help me move the piano. He said, "Move it yourself."

The words, "Nigger, you fool," flew out of my mouth.

For an instant, I saw fire come from his body. He started shuddering and pointing his finger at me. He said, "You, you come with me." I was surprised because I had no idea what was going on. We lived in the country and my parents had never told us about the hardship of blacks growing up during that time. We did not have a TV in our early years, so we had no idea what was happening in the cities and states around us. My parents taught that us we should love everyone. No matter who came to our house, my parents treated them the same.

In our day, parents taught us to respect adults. Our community helped to raise all children. This meant that if you did something wrong, your neighbor would give you a spanking. When your parents got home, you got another spanking to make sure you learned your lesson. If a teacher said something, parents were eager to correct the problem, which meant another spanking. At the time children did not have a voice, only a behind to spank. Mr. Brown said, "You come with me." He walked so fast that I could barely keep up.

All the while I kept saying, "I was just joking the way you joke with us. What did I say that was so wrong?"

I repeated this over and over; but Mr. Brown would only say, "Come on, come with me." When we got into his office, he called my Aunt Jane, who ran the store beside the school. He told her what I had said. Right then and there, I knew my life was over. I felt like I was on fire, for Mr. Brown had done the thing all children in our school were terrified of — he called my parents (telling Aunt Jane was like telling my parents).

I do not remember too much of the rest of the day because all I could think about was what was going to happen to me when Dad and Mom got home. On the bus ride home, I asked my cousin Mary if she would run away with me before Dad got home. I told her what had happened, as if I needed to, as the whole school was talking about it. My dad was going to beat me to death. My heart was already beating out of my chest.

Mary, being a faithful cousin, said, "Yes, I will." Dad worked second shift, so he would not get home until late. My mom was so upset she feared laying a hand on me and told me Dad was going to handle it. When night fell, I got a few things together and walked over to Mary's house. She came outside and gave the okay. We only got about two blocks before Mary started crying about how her mom was going to miss her. Maybe her mom would have a heart attack when she discovered her gone. She cried so much that I relented.

"Okay, let's just run away and get on the school bus my brother drives." In some place in my mind, I thought that Dad would miss me so much and fear for my life that he would forget about the beating he was going to give me. What a fool I was for thinking such a fantasy! Even when I think about it today, I think, "What a fool!"

When Dad got home, he came into the room that the six of us slept in. When he and Mom couldn't find me anywhere in the house, they called the neighbors together. About an hour or two later, we heard all the neighbors gather together to start looking for us. Mary and I had gotten on the bus beside our house. Someone said, "Hey let's start by looking on the bus."

My ears started to burn and I said to myself, "Here we go." One of the neighbors got on the bus and then yelled out to my dad that we were found. All I remember was a belt coming down and my dad saying, "I am going to give you something to run away for!" Dad made sure Mary and I both got some licks on the bus. He then beat me in front of the neighbors. I remember saying, "Dad, please let me explain." What did I say that for? Saying it alone must have added ten extra licks. Dad took me in the house. By this time all my brothers and sisters were awake. Dad hit me, and I started hitting him back. I was like a wild animal, caged up and fighting for my life. I remember getting my licks in with my dad; but he, being the stronger, got the best of me. He beat me until he was exhausted and couldn't hit me anymore. I was 15 years old when this happened. I resolved that I would not speak to him again. I remember him going to bed. Little did I know that he almost beat himself into a heart attack.

You would think this would be enough. However, when I went to school the next day, Mr. Brown decided there would be hell to pay for saying those horrible, sickening words to him. He started by having me fired from the cafeteria. In those days, if your family's income fell within a certain bracket, students could work around the school. Then as the days went on, he started to harass me. I tried to tell him I meant no harm, but no matter how much I apologized, he kept picking on me. At the time, I wasn't talking to my dad. If he came in a room, I left. I talked to my mom about it. She realized I had meant no harm, I just hadn't known any better, and I had made an innocent mistake. I told her how bad it had gotten with Mr. Brown and how I was afraid to go to school. She then talked about it with my dad. Dad went out to the school to have a conference with Mr. Brown. Afterwards, the teacher stopped picking on me. Deep in my soul, Dad had become my hero; for he saved my life that day.

Over 30 years later, as I sit down at my parent's breakfast table reading them this chapter, I can feel all kinds of memories coming back for them. I look up to see my daddy crying. My mom, with tears in her own eyes, starts talking to me about where my dad had come from. The Lord had brought him a mighty long way.

Mom told me something I do not hear too often today. From the first day she saw my dad, she fell in love with him and decided she wanted to spend the rest of her life with him. She told me my dad had come from his own bad place in life. He had a mom who treated him like the black sheep in the family. He got frequent beatings. He was always the first in line when something was done wrong in the family. She said my dad felt so unloved by his mom. Even when Mom met her, my grandmother's unloving heart was still there. She spoke of how my grandmother thought my mother was too good for my dad and told her so. She also talked of how my grandmother encouraged her to go out and party when my dad was out. She told my mom that two could play the game of partying.

My mom hastened to tell me that she decided her children were more important than partying to get even, so many nights she stayed home and prayed for help.

Mom says my dad had at least one person in his corner who helped him through his childhood, his grandmother. She would talk to him and help him see the good in himself. She lifted him up. When he needed financial help, she would be there. These hard things taught Dad to love his children equally and not show favoritism to any of us. It's funny as I think about this because each of us feels like Dad's favorite. Good can always come from evil if allowed to. I had a conversation with my grandmother several years before she died. My sisters and I had talked about how unloved we felt by our grandmother on Daddy's side. She always treated us as if we were hand-me-down grandkids. Her preference was always for her daughters' children, and she made sure we knew our place.

When we got older, I could not let it go, so I confronted her. I asked her if she had ever loved us. I told her how she had made us feel. I could see in her eyes she hadn't meant to make us feel that way. Like so many of us, she was young and only knew the life that was before her. She said she had always loved us. Right then I could see something in her change. Life does that. It takes away the bitter if you let it and replaces it with kindness, gentleness, and love. She warmed up to me, and we talked for a long time. I asked her about my granddad and how long they had been married before my aunt was born. She quickly saw where I was going and told me that children should not ask grown-ups questions. I told her humbly that if everything stayed a secret, then our past would be lost as the generations passed away. Funny, she never answered my question, but she did tell me that when she and Granddad got married, he would go out all the time. She said she also went out to party and drink with him. She could hang with the best of them, but she said after a while she gave up the bottle because she realized that one of them had to be there to raise the kids. From that day on, my grandmother and I have had a loving relationship. I felt like I understood her a lot better. I could tell she accepted my brothers, sisters, and me as her grandchildren. I have often thought that because of the partying and clubbing, it is easier for a mom to accept her daughter's children as her grandchildren because they come from her daughter's body. Depending on their upbringing, they might find it harder to accept their son's children because there was always a chance the woman could have fooled around on their son.

My parents both say that before my grandmother died, they had made amends with her. I could see, in my dad's tone, the love and respect he learned to have for her. How many years were wasted on pain that could have been worked out if only they had known how to talk about it? But is it any different today? Instead of thinking the best first about each other, so many people think the worst. By thinking the worst first, one closes themselves off to hearing the other person's side. There are always two sides to every story. When we see things through our own selfish eyes, it makes it hard to open ourselves to the other person's side. How many divorces have happened because somebody told someone about their spouse and that spouse believed the person without getting both sides of the story?

Then I thought, maybe my grandmother had felt this way because my dad had been dating my mom and another woman at the same time. In fact, both had had my dad's children only months apart from each other. My dad ultimately chose my mom, and they got married ten months after my oldest sister was born.

My mom never called my other sister, Dale, our half-sister or stepsister. Mom said it carries the idea of something not worthy of being a true part of the family, only an unfortunate part or a regret. My mom said, "children are innocent and should not be mistreated because of decisions made by their parents." Little did I know how much these words would shape me in the future.

Mom would have Dale over to spend lots of time with us. Dale had been a sickly child most of her life, a special needs child who mentally would never go beyond a fifth grade education. When she was in her early twenties, she got very sick and went into the hospital. We were told we would go to see her soon. We children really wanted to visit, but one evening we got a phone call from the hospital telling us that she had passed away. We did not even get to say good-bye. The whole family mourned her. The memory still brings tears to my eyes as I remember the sister whom we all lost. To this day, my mom and Dale's mom are close friends. They have given us a huge example of forgiveness and living out forgiveness. It would have been so easy for my mom to hate the competition, but she chose to love instead. Our lives were all the better for it.

I am glad that Mom instilled this quality in me. When I was growing up, I did not want to be anything like my mom. She gave 90% of the discipline. I had a great dislike for it and for her handing it out while I was growing up. I now see that I am just like my mom, and I find myself proud of it.

My parents asked me about my abuse. Why did I not tell them when it happened? I can see my dad blames himself. I explain that at the time, I had been told it was my fault, and I had believed it. My dad said that maybe it was best that I hadn't told him because he might have killed Devil Man and then he would not have been there for us. They start to talk about how two of my other sisters had been abused by my mom's brother and how they had not found out about the abuse until my sisters were grown. It's sad that none of us even talked about our situation to each other. We could have found comfort and healing if we only had known. Instead, as with most silent killers, this one ran its course. All three of us went down very self-destructive roads. I developed a longing for the sexual stimulation. It was so confusing to me when I was abused, yet I felt I needed love from a man no matter the cost to me. My sisters developed a dependency on alcohol in the need to forget their pain at all cost to them.

When I spoke to both of my sisters recently about this book, I told them I wanted to tell their story. They both agreed that they did not want all the details of their life published, but they did want everyone to know that they neither drink nor feel the need to drink today to feel fulfilled and happy.

Recently, my younger sister decided she wanted to share a few things that had happened to her. She remembered feeling so shy. She could not even talk to other people. One day she took a drink and felt like a weight had been lifted off her. She was able to talk, joke, and laugh with others. She thought drinking a little helped take the edge off, so that's what she did. She did not realize that over a period of time, she required more and more alcohol to get the same feeling. Once, she remembered waking up with a guy and not even knowing how she got there. The next thing she knew she was pregnant but did not have a clue who the father was. She said, "I was so ashamed. I did not want to bring a baby into this world and not even be able to tell it where it came from or who its daddy was. So, I did what I thought was best, I had an abortion. I thought I could just forget and go on, but I could not. I started to drink even more. I fooled myself and everyone else. They thought I was drinking just to have fun. They had no idea that I was drinking to forget myself and the bad choices I had made."

I asked my sister what made her stop and when she realized she had had enough of the lifestyle. She reminded me of the time when our brother was visiting from Washington, and she went to my parents to pick up his three children. She had been drinking before she left home but was able to disguise it when she got to my parents' home. On her way home, she had a car accident. The children thankfully survived. She had some cuts and bruises but the biggest hurt was the fact that she could have killed those children. That was her eye-opening moment. She did not want to live her whole life in a drunken stupor. She did not want to hurt others — even her own children — and then try to live with it. She decided to pray, get counseling, and put the bottle down for good. On the day of the accident, she not only lost her many reasons for drinking but her husband as well. He had had his fill with her drinking and left.

Both my sisters remind me so much of my dad. They made a decision that drinking wasn't what they were looking for. It just covered the pain until they could find it. The cost, all the pain they and their families went through, was too much. They both live happy lives now because they have been granted a second chance.

My parents wanted me to read Chapter One to them, but I told them that I could not. I just didn't have it in me. My dad gently asked, "It's going to be in the book, so why won't you read it to us?" I told them that if I read it, they would cry when they heard about the events. I could not bear to see that pain on their faces. I told them how helpless I had felt all those years ago, and I did not want to take them to that place. I did tell them I would pull Chapter One up on my computer to let them read it for themselves. I hope they didn't but, being a parent myself, I know they did.

Would Anyone Cry For Me?

Three

Broken Promises, He Loves Me, He Loves Me Not

When I began high school, I was very shy. My family would not agree since to them I was the family joker. The family did not start having fun until I joined in. I could not understand myself. The person I wanted to be looked just like the person my family thought I was. The person living inside me was very different. She still could not be alone with any man, not even my father. He had done nothing but love me and I could not be alone in the same room with him.

I also picked up another habit; I became a tattletale. Tattling became my way of asking for attention when the words would not come out. I believe it was because of my shame and my blaming myself for what had happened.

None of my siblings would let me hang out with them. They did all the cool stuff such as smoking and drinking. I would have none of it. They knew I would tell on them so they left me alone in my own world. I do not even remember having any real friends. Did I? I truly do not remember.

One day I was in class, looking out the window, when I saw the most handsome young man. With each step he took, he looked like a young rabbit hopping along. He was tall and thin with caramel skin, curly sandy colored hair, and lips fit for kissing. In an instant, I fell for this stranger. Somehow, I had to find out his name. Was someone the desire of his eyes already? Would he talk to me and be my friend? For the first time, something in me was unafraid. I could not explain my feeling, but I wanted to find out who this young boy was. I think I asked someone in class who he was in a seemingly uncaring way. His name was James. His father was a teacher at the next school we would attend. I also found out he played football. My new plan was made. I decided that if I was to meet him, I needed to stay after school. The school was having girl basketball tryouts soon. I asked my parents if I could try out. They said yes and a dream was born. The first day after tryouts, I knew parents would be picking up their kids at my Aunt Jane's store next door. I hurried over there. When I saw him, he looked even better up close. I spoke to him and quickly walked away. This went on for several days. Finally, he stopped me to start up a conversation. James told me he really liked me and wanted us to be friends. I thought I had died and gone to heaven. We talked every day after school while try-outs were going on.

One day, he did it. He kissed me. There was nothing more inviting in my world than James. The next day, he kissed me again. This time was no different than the first. I knew I wanted him to be mine. It blew my mind how just weeks before I was afraid of men; and now, I desired this young man.

Disaster struck. He told me he liked another girl, and he had asked her to be his girlfriend. He told me he did not know what was happening between us, but he needed to give her a chance to give him an answer first. The news was like a knife cutting off a piece of unwanted meat. My heart was twisted up and thrown in the trash. How could he give me a kiss of death like that? Did he not know that we were meant for each other? This girl could never care about him the way that I did. If she had, she would not have to think about being his girl. I was devastated. Needless to say, I did not make the team. Life became just like it was before, empty.

One day when we were changing classes, the man of my dreams came running up to me to tell me he and this girl had broken up. James said he wanted me to be his new girlfriend. What I did not know was that he wanted to have intimate relations with this girl, but she had told him no. In his anger, he told her if she would not, then I would. By spitting out these words to her, James, of course, had insulted her. She broke it off with him. I do not know if I would have changed my mind even if I had known he had said this. My teenage heart felt like a caged animal in heat. James had the key to open the door to let me out. At the time, I thought it was so honorable that he would give her a chance after he had met and kissed me. I knew nothing about the character of a young hormone-driven teen boy. In my mind, James was so fine and handsome I didn't even care. We started to be an item from that moment on. Dreams of the future danced in my head. I thought I could finally put to rest my past. How could I put to rest a past that was also my present and, for a time, my future?

It was some time before kissing turned into touching and touching into more. I remember the day I first gave myself to him. At no point did I feel like I was a virgin because of my past. I still thought what happened was my fault. I had not breathed a word about it to anyone. That is, until James came into my life. At some point, I told him what had happened and how I feared all men. Instead of saying it was my fault, he told me he would protect me and no more harm would come my way. I had never felt safer. Nor had I ever known what love was until that moment.

Our first time... how did it happen and who wanted it the most? James and I had talked about how we wanted to be together and how beautiful it would be. We fantasized about the day we would first be intimate. In time, we decided to put our need, our desire, our lust for each other into action. James picked me up and told me that we were going to his parents' home. I thought his parents would be in but we were alone. In so many ways, I believed I wanted it more than James. We went to his room and started kissing. He touched me and, before I knew it, my breast was in his hand. He caressed me and kissed me. He took off my clothes and soon his hands were softly probing. They felt so warm and at that time I had never felt so protected. I let him put me on his bed. He climbed on top of me. I felt him become aroused, and it was welcomed by me. I thought it would not hurt; but the intimacy did. When I moaned in pain, James stopped for a moment to allow me to get comfortable before we tried again. After a few more tries, we had success. I thought, "Now a woman is born." After that first time, James and I were intimate wherever and whenever we could. It was wonderful. I could not get enough of him. All that mattered was being together and satisfying the desire we had for each other. James was my only true friend. It did not matter if no one else wanted to hang out with me because he did. He was my whole world, but all fantasy worlds must drift back into reality.

I felt funny one day, kind of sick to my stomach at the smell of breakfast. What could be wrong? I had never felt like this before. I did not want to tell anyone so I kept it to myself. The next day, it happened again. Being young and uneducated in the ways of the world, I did not know that I had just stepped into womanhood. I talked to James about what was happening and we decided to take a test to see if I was pregnant. Somehow, we got a pregnancy kit and waited for the results. A minute later, the reality of what we had been doing in the dark came into the light. We were going to be parents. I thought now everyone would know what we had been doing. Now, the other kids at school would know what kind of girl I was — no good, just a toy for men to play with. I think I cried for a little while, but James told me not to worry. We would figure it out. I do not think he gave me any comfort that day. A day or so later, James called in a panic. He said we had to end the pregnancy because his father would be ridiculed if word got out at school. His position as a teacher at my high school would make him the target of gossip.

Immediately my mind jumped back to what had happened to me as a child. How I had prayed over and over that Devil Man would pay for what he had done to me! After he died in the car accident, I blamed myself for his death. Now, I was told by the young man I loved that I must voluntarily kill my unborn baby. Fear gripped me as I went into shut down mode. How could I hurt James and his family? More than that, how could I kill our unborn baby? I did not know what to do. Yet, even at the time, I knew there was not going to be any type of winning situation. I was going to lose no matter which way I went. I was going to lose James or lose my child. The world would never look the same. I would never be the same. Oh, if only I had waited until I was older. If only I had been more careful. If I could've of, would've of, should've but that was not my reality. My reality was making a decision a young teenage girl should never have to make. The decision was to kill my baby or to kill my heart. James and I talked about this for weeks. Finally, when I had no more strength to argue, I told him I would end the pregnancy. Life as I knew it was over. The young woman staring back at me in the mirror started to become a dark, evil stranger. Now, in my own eyes, I was a murderer, a liar, a deceiver, and worthless. Darkness surrounded me and twisted me into a loop of depression deeper than anything I had known before. That was it. There was no more good left in me. I gave myself away, and I was on my way to getting used up. What did I care? There was nothing left worth saving.

James and I went to an abortion clinic in town. I do not know how we got the money to pay for the abortion but we did. The green cash was my gun. I was about to fire it into the doctor's hand and kill the innocence of my unborn child. I do not think I thought that day. I just survived. It was as if I was in a trance looking down on a girl I did not know. A girl who did one of the things she had told herself she would never do. When you are broken, you find yourself taking off pieces of yourself and throwing them into the trash can of your own heart. I kept telling myself the abortion was needed in order for me to survive and keep my boyfriend, but the minute it was over, everything in me told me I was a murderer. How could I ask for forgiveness when I had known it was wrong before I did it?

To make matters worse, James wanted to have me in his arms and in his bed. He treated me as if we had not just killed our baby. Who was this man I was looking at? Where did he come from? Who invited him into my world? Oh, that's right, me! Thank goodness he could not touch me for several weeks. But like an alcoholic with liquor, I was addicted to how he made me feel. I cut out another piece of myself and put in on the shelf with the other hurt and pain. I packed it in my suitcase of self-hate and destruction.

Over 30 years later, I decided to find out James' side of the story. I shared with him what the abortion had done to me and how I had felt afterwards. I told him how I had felt about him wanting me. He replied, "You were right. I did want to be intimate with you the day of the abortion. All my life, when I feel hurt, pain, anger, or joy, I like to be in the arms of someone who loves me. This makes me know someone other than I cares about me and loves me. It brings me peace and calm. It helps me survive when I am going through the toughest times in my life. What we did was one of the toughest things I have ever had to do in my life." He continued, "I think about what we did even to this day. I have never gotten over it. I have just learned how to live with it. It's been hard to forgive myself. Sometimes, I am not sure that I have, but I know that I cannot change that decision. I can only grow from it." Finally, his words brought me some peace. I now know I was not the only one hurt and changed by the decision.

I cried alone most of this time because I had to bear my new pain alone. I could not tell James what I was feeling because it had started as his idea and my decision. I did not want to lose him after I had just lost the child we would have shared. I did the one thing I knew how to do. I went to God in prayer and asked for terms of forgiveness. I started by telling God what I had done and how utterly empty I felt. It had been my decision, no matter how much pressure I had been under. I took full responsibility for my actions. I asked Him to watch over my little baby that was in heaven with Him. Then I asked for something that would again change the course of my life. I asked God for another child, one who would take the place of the one I had killed. I told Him I would love this new child and would not let harm come his way. I told God that if He granted me this one thing, I would sacrifice my womb and not expect any more children. I had wanted lots of children, but my punishment would be to only have the one from my body.

I started scheming to get pregnant again. I could not let

James know my intentions. It was my only goal. I was too blind to see that he was moving on and wanted to see what life, as well as other girls, had to offer him. I did not even care that a part of me was changing as well. All I could see was my desire to make a wrong right. My mother always said, "Two wrongs do not make a right," but I thought I knew better. She and her words were old and outdated. Every time I had the opportunity, I gave myself to James. I did not know that when I accepted my high school diploma, I was already with child. When I got pregnant, no one was happier than I. I could not see my life beyond this baby, so I did not know what the cost would be to both me and to my son. The true price would only be revealed many years later. I had no symptoms. I thought life was good.

Foolishly and through blinded eyes, I thought God had answered my prayers, but like in the fantasy world of make believe, I was wrong. God would not have placed the burden of being a single mom on me. No, I had placed this on myself, and believe me, there was hell to pay for all of us.

I told James about the baby. On his face, I think I saw two things — happiness and disbelief. Maybe, in some way, he felt as guilty as I had after killing our unborn baby. I told him that no matter what, this child would have life. He must have seen my resolve because he did not try to talk me out of it. Now came the hard part, telling our parents.

Because of my childhood, the only way I could handle pressure was to mentally block out the pain and to make a joke about the rest. Laughter was my biggest deception. I even deceived myself with it. James and I decided to tell my parents first. We wanted to see if I had a home to live in once the news was out.

We asked my parents if we could talk to them and we all went into the living room. Before James could get the story out, I started smiling, gently laughing, and could not wipe the grin off

my face. When James finally finished, I could see that my parents'
dream of breaking the cycle of premarital pregnancy had failed.
I felt as if I had brought shame into our family and disgrace to
our name. We dared not tell our parents that this was not our first
pregnancy. An already bad situation would have been made even
worse. We told them that we would respect any decision they
made when it came to my living with them during my pregnancy
and after the baby was born. My parents are people of mercy and
allowed me to stay. They knew I had nowhere to go. They did not
see it as my failing them. They believed that they had failed me,
which was the farthest thing from the truth. My parents had raised
us to know right from wrong; but because I had wanted to live my
own life, I did not care about the consequences. I did not listen. I
know I was ashamed. My dad and I did not really speak again until
months later when the baby was born. I would not know for over
15 years that my dad was crushed because of where he saw my life
heading— where a single mom's life usually heads. Silence was
the way he and I chose to handle the pain.

It was the circle of human life, starting again with me. A
child is born, depending entirely on her parents for life, trusting
they will care for her. The child grows and imitates them, but
around the teenage years, the child thinks she is an adult. Then the
child thinks she knows more than her parents. The child lives life
on her own terms, gets pregnant, and another child is born. Only
when the circle starts over, do we realize that our parents knew
best.

We had a little different reaction from James' parents. His
mom's response was, "Oh my God, Betty's pregnant! None of
my other boys did this to me. They all had children after they got
married." His dad said, "Son, you are going to take care of this
child, even if you have to quit school. You will take care of your
responsibility." They did say they would accept our child into the
family. How difficult that must have been for James to hear, but we
got through it.

What I did not know was that James had thought that I had been seeing another guy. He thought that maybe this child was not his. I found this out some twenty years later. When he first told me, I was devastated by how much time had been lost of him truly loving his son. Secondly, I wondered why he had not had a DNA test done when he first begin doubting. I suggested he should get a DNA test done now for his own peace of mind even though our son looks completely like him. Finally, I told him I had never fooled around on him. I had valued him and our relationship as much as my mom had valued my dad. I explained that my love for him was true. I had never even looked at other young men when we dated. How much pain we could have prevented if the two of us had sat down and gotten both sides of the story from each other? The one who suffered the most was our son. James had told me that he had gotten over those thoughts years ago. He just wanted to share where he was at the time.

Our son, baby Vent Syrell, was the most beautiful child who had ever been created. Born at 12:37AM on January 27, 1982, he had ten fingers, ten toes, and the loudest, healthiest cry you could ask for. I promised myself that this child would not be harmed and that no one would take away his innocence the way Devil Man had taken away mine. I wanted everything to be perfect for our son. I even had natural childbirth. James and my mom took me to the hospital. Since we thought I would be there for a very long time, I encouraged Mom to go home, get some rest, and come back early the next morning. James stayed with me at the hospital. I believed all was well. I did not know that I had already lost James' eyes. He was already looking for a new adventure. But how could I blame this very young man who was in his senior year of high school? At that age, "the grass always looks greener on the other side."

Ever since we had told my parents I was pregnant, my dad did not have much if anything to say to me. I knew he was hurt, and there was no way I could take away his pain. I had broken his trust and his heart. Mom said that only time would tell if our relationship could be mended.

Early in the morning after the baby was born, we called our parents to tell them they were now grandparents to a healthy boy. I was on cloud nine but just a little sad that my mom was not there when Syrell was born.

My mom came by to see us early on her way to work. It made me very happy, but what made me the happiest was when my dad came up later in the day. As he talked to me, both of us knew that all was forgiven. We played cards together, talking and talking. My dad, my hero, was back.

A few days later, we took the baby home. The lesson of life began. All I can remember of the first few weeks was the crying and the lack of sleep. My mom believed if you make your bed hard, you must lie in it.

She let me learn the hard way that being a mom was more than just having a baby. I don't know how long this went on. I do remember one night as the baby was crying, I could not get up to care for him. I started to cry. My mom came in the room and said, "I got him tonight; get some sleep." I must have fallen into a near coma because all I remember of the rest of the night was that I had the best and most caring mom ever. After getting sleep, I was able to take care of Syrell from then on. Knowing my mom was there if things got too stressful was a big comfort.

Months went by; it was evident that James and I were through. He came around a little to see the baby but anything more than that was just a dream on my part. The final straw came one day when I went to his house so that his parents could visit with Syrell. I was really going to be nosy and see if I could figure out what was going on with him. I made up a reason to go in his room. I looked in one of his nightstand drawers and that's when I saw it,

a girl in her sexy lingerie, posing for pictures for him. I became
sick to my stomach and decided that I no longer needed to flip
on the James button of self-destruction. I had had my fill. In fact,
my cup had run over. I had fooled myself into believing that he
had given me the one thing I wanted and needed. Now that I had
Syrell, James' job was over. There is nothing like a woman who
feels scorned. I decided then and there that I would inflict the same
massive pain on him that he had inflicted on me. I did not know
when, where, or how; but I knew, oh boy, did I know, that I would
even the pain scale. On that day, as much as I had loved him in our
past, I hated him.

I held the tears back as I finished visiting with his parents.
There was no way that I would give them any inkling that I had
snooped or that I had gotten what I was looking for. I think I went
numb for a while. I did not want to move forward or backward.
I only wanted love and knew I had none. I cried for myself, but I
thought to myself, "Would anyone cry for me?" I needed a friend,
but I had lost him. I did not want to go on. However, I must go on
because the baby needed me: and I needed him.

James soon married and left to find a life for his family.
I rarely heard from him. When I did, it was always on his time.
One Christmas, James called to say he wanted to get Syrell so he
could spend time with his other family. Nicely, I told him it would
be okay. When he came to pick Syrell up, I could see that he still
desired me. It was like we were back in our school days. I took him
to another room and gave myself to him. As I allowed him to have
me, I was already planning my next move. He kept telling me how
much he longed for what we used to have. I whispered to him that
I longed for it also. I knew I was committing adultery, and love
was the farthest thing from my mind. My joy and smile weren't
because I had my love back. They were because I would now
inflict the heart-breaking pain of betrayal. I kissed him. He told me
everything would be all right somehow. I told him "of course," and
I meant it.

When James had taken his family back home a few states away, I put my plan in motion. I knew how I would seek my revenge. Where do we get these demon thoughts and plans from? Hell itself must be the place, for only pure evil could do this thing I had planned out for James. At that point in my life, no one could have talked me out of it. I survived purely to inflict my poison on him and in him. My first step was to write a very guilty yet innocent letter to James about not wanting to break up his family. The love we had made would linger in my heart always but I knew we could never be. I apologized for loving him and sprayed it with perfume. I knew if his wife saw it she might not open it. There was only a 50/50 chance and I couldn't have that. Satan whispered in my ear that perfume would do the trick. It would change that 50/50 chance to a 100% slam-dunk. I addressed it, put a stamp on it, and mailed off my poison.

I went on as if nothing had happened. I even felt a little freer. A few days later, I got a phone call from James. He whispered to me that everything was going to be okay for us. I started laughing to myself because I knew my plan had succeeded. I yelled silently to myself, "Who's your play thing now?" His wife got on the phone and started yelling. She told me I needed to worry about my own life and to stay out of theirs. I told her I was not the one who had married her or made her all kinds of commitments. The person she needed to be talking to was right there in the room with her and his name started with a "J". As we hung up the phone, I felt like a weight of hatred had been lifted off my shoulders and placed on theirs. Why did I have to hurt this woman? She had done nothing to me personally, but I had determined in my heart that she was as much my enemy as James. Any friend of James' was an enemy of mine. Later in life, I would feel the same hurt she did when my husband decided that he longed for a different version of me.

Would Anyone Cry For Me?

Four

Playing Grown-up as a Teen Age Mom

After the break-up with James, I began to focus on myself and my needs. I forgot that I had made a commitment to love and care for my son at all cost. Pain and self-preservation have a way of making you forget promises. I was more of my father's child than I could see. I had hated that he was not home with us when we were young, yet that is what I began to do to my son. I didn't understand myself. The things I did not want to do, I did.

I wanted to find happiness. Staying at home was not the answer. How would the man I desired know I even existed if I did not go out and show myself? How could I find love behind closed doors? I started partying whenever I could. The clubbing and spending time with my girlfriends took me to the next stage in my life.

I had never wanted to be a party girl; but at the age of 20, my life just seemed to evolve and make me into one. I did realize that my heart was so broken and torn that if I focused on it, I found I could not breathe. I had given myself and trusted so much in James that I had lost the little of me I still had. The pain was so great that I had to cover it with the pretend heart of another man. Someone, anyone, to love me and make me feel special. When I was getting myself pregnant, I never imagined I would feel so empty. I wanted to be the kind of mother my mom was. I wanted my child to know he could depend on me. Pain is a mighty heavy tool that will make you do unheard of things to relieve it. My heart hurt and I only wanted to find peace and happiness. I knew it wasn't at home because I had no one to share my life with. I was so lost in my own needs that I forgot about the needs of my son. I hurt so much I could not see how much I was hurting my son or myself.

I gathered around friends who were like me — girls who wanted to find a way out of the unhappiness of their sad life, girls who missed peace and fulfillment and wanted to find it, girls who had dreams about their futures and fantasies about their reality.

My friends were young and empty just like me. We got along great together. We were the very picture of misery loves company. We knew we just needed a plan to find happiness and the men who would give it to us.

My girlfriends and I decided we would all meet at one house to get ready to go out partying. We knew we wanted to let our hair hang down, so we put on the make-up of make believe. We wore the smiles of a clown.

No one was happier than we were. Our dresses were tight. Our attitude was intimidating. No one could see the true us: just the make-believe masks.

I sometimes wonder how much things have changed in the world. Then I realize that times change and technology changes; but the character of man is the same, no matter what the year is. We all want to feel loved, noticed, appreciated, needed, and important. If we can't get those feelings by natural means, then we look to the next best place, our pretend reality. You know the warmth of our smiles, the seduction of our walk, and the arrogance of our demeanor. The emptiness affects all people in one way or another. From the wealthiest to the poorest, our pocketbooks may allow us to handle it differently, but love, loneliness, and pain are the same across the spectrum.

We started the evening with a small cocktail to shake off the day. Then we proceeded to get ready. No one could tell us we were not "the cat's meow." As I fantasized about the evening, I gave no thought to the responsibility I was leaving for my parents to handle.

We walked into the club as if we owned it. I saw him, the new guy of my fantasy. I moved close to him so he could recognize what he had been missing in life. As he caught my eyes, I turned away as if shy. In a small way I was shy, but by now I knew what I was doing. I was leading him into longing for me. I wanted him to want me. I would stop at nothing until I got what I wanted.

I could tell he was a breed apart. He was a student from the University and was studying medicine. He wanted more than his degree. He wanted his green card. I wanted someone to love me. When we talked, we discovered that we were born in two different parts of the world on the same day and year. I thought it was a match meant to be. We dated for a short period. Sex was quickly introduced into our relationship. He did everything to make me feel like he really cared, and I bought it all. How fragile was my broken heart that I would buy any words of admiration spoken to me. It was easy to forget he wanted something from me as much as I wanted him. He laid the trap well. He needed to get married and get a green card, or he would have to leave me. I was surely not going to lose the new guy in my life. He was only the second guy I had dated, but I couldn't be without him. Believing we could make the marriage work, I told him I would marry him. I was planning a marriage, and I didn't even know if he would truly accept my son.

I did not even look to see if he even acted like he liked children. In fact, things happened so fast that I did not notice how he did not want to be around my son. A part of me may have kept my son from him in order to make sure he was protected. The only thing I did right was to protect my son from the pain of abuse. I only let him spend time with immediate family members and Rosa, his god-mom.

One day we sneaked off to get married. In the back of my mind, I thought I could put all the pieces of wife and motherhood in one place. We did not tell anyone at first that we were married. I would spend the days and afternoons with him before going home to my parents at night. This lasted a few months until the evening I fell asleep at his place and did not wake up until the next day. That's when I knew we had to tell my parents because they did not play around. The rule was that their house was not a revolving door; and while under their roof, we lived by their rules. They told us that whenever we wanted to make the rules it would be okay with them. We just needed to find our own place. I knew they meant it. So, I told my husband he needed to man up and tell my parents we were married. I reassured him that my parents were very understanding; and if it came from him, they would respect it.

I truly believed my parents asked themselves who I was. I was the worst mom, not spending time with my own child for some man. I got married out of the blue and just expected everyone to live with it. I know without a doubt they prayed for me frequently. I am so glad they never gave up on me.

My parents decided to announce our marriage by giving us a wedding reception. I knew my husband did not want this, but he had to go along with it in order to get what he wanted. We were both biding our time for our own needs. He and I moved into a small one-bedroom apartment while I left my son to be raised by my parents. I knew, in many ways, they could give him what I did not have time for. They could provide the unconditional love I had promised. I was too busy looking for my own love and sacrificing anything to get it. Over the course of the next ten months, I visited my son frequently. Life at home with my husband was beginning to show itself for what it was which was nothing. My husband started spending more and more time at the university, even spending the night. I knew in my heart what was going on, but I just wouldn't look at reality. I knew that if I did it would all come tumbling down. This new fantasy world would be over. I went along with it for as long as I could. I remembered my mom and thought, "Time will tell what reality is." I was willing to stick it out and go the distance, but that was not my husband's plan. Things were getting worse and worse. One day, I broke into an old black briefcase he kept locked. I saw the love letters of the woman who had stolen his heart. She wrote all kinds of sweet nothings to him. I remembered breaking the heart of an innocent woman; I had not given a second thought to how she felt. I had only thought about myself and fulfilling my vengeance, fueled by my hatred and rage. Now, I knew how it felt to be the wife on the other side of the situation. I knew my husband had promised to love and honor me. I also knew that his words were just empty promises.

When I saw his green card as well, I decided enough was enough. I took his green card and the keys to my car to hide them. I knew he would be very upset. I wanted to be able to get away in a hurry if I needed to. I waited all evening for him to come home. When he finally did, it was very late. When he came in, I told him I needed to talk to him. He replied he was going back out to study. When he went in the room and saw his briefcase busted open, he became enraged. He looked for his green card. I told him he would never see it or me again.

He attacked me. He knocked me down onto the floor, slapping me and choking me. I could feel the air go out of my lungs but I could not feel a breath coming back in. It took everything I had to break away from him. He asked me, "Where is my stuff?" This was an "aha" moment. I knew he meant business. Sensing that my life was in danger, I told him it was in the bedroom, in the top dresser drawer, to the left, and in the back. He let me go and ran to get his belongings. Knowing this was my only chance to get away, I ran to the door, grabbed the keys and green card I had hidden in a bowl beside the door, and I ran for my life. I jumped in the car and quickly locked the doors. He ran down to the car and began beating on the door, demanding I open it. I told him it would be a cold day in hell when I would do what he told me to do again. I started the car and sped off to the safety of my parents' home. When I got there, I broke down and told them what was going on. It took all of my energy to get away and then tell my story. After crying a while, I realized all I had left was hurt, shame, depression, and exhaustion.

I was broken. At this point, I felt like life itself was not worth living. I toyed for days with the notion that no one would miss me if I were not around. Then my husband called to say he wanted a divorce. I had no more strength. I decided to end my life and my sorrows. I was in a dark hole with no light. I did not know which way was up and which way was down. I could not see past the here and the now. No matter what anyone whispered to me, all I could hear was "bad girl, bad mom, and bad life." I was in a room filled with family members; and yet, I felt alone. My heart felt like someone had wrapped it in a chain with an unbearable weight, locked it, and threw away the key. I prayed to God to help me make the right decision. Then I took a handful of pills and told God my life was in His hands. I went to sleep not knowing where I would waken. All I knew was that wherever it was, it would be better than the here and now.

When I first opened my eyes, I was disappointed to still be alive. After thinking about it, I concluded that God must have a purpose for me and would one day reveal it to me.

I made a commitment to myself then that no man would break my heart again the way James and my husband had. I became what I call pure evil: a woman who wanted love but who would not give it. I really wanted someone to just come along and love, protect, and value me, but I put that in my little black box of disappointments and glued it shut. Everything about me changed on the inside again. I told myself I would never completely give in to a man again. No one would ever own all of me. I was so empty. I felt like a dead dog, useless. I was the only one who knew this about me. The rest of the world just saw my pretense, the me of my own dreams.

I was planning to have this be a small chapter without all the dark details that happened after my divorce. I was concerned about showing you an even darker, baser side of me but how can I show you the true Betty if you do not know all of me?

After my husband and I divorced, I tried to deal with the

pain. I went to Miles to see if he could help me understand what had happened. I needed someone to talk to. He went to school with my husband. I had thought he was a nice, respectable, young man. When I got there, he was glad to see me. We talked and I told him my side of the story. He told me my husband was a fool and that he would regret treating me with such contempt. He was being really nice to me and then he hugged me. I thought the caress was for comfort, but he had so much more in mind. The next thing I knew, he was kissing me and telling me my husband did not know what he was giving up. Those words of comfort made me feel so wanted and needed that I allowed him to have me. I felt two things. The first was revenge on my husband. The other emotion was that someone noticed me. It wasn't until afterwards that I wished that I had just stayed home that evening.

I decided to stay away from Miles so that I could get my head together. I went to another friend of my husband, Sun. He was a very intelligent guy, cute, and nerdy at the same time. He was kind, sweet, and comforting. We went to dinner and just hung out for a while. But like Miles, he wanted me as well. He was a little different; he took his time. He did not rush me. He wooed me into bed. He told me he wanted to comfort me, help me, and relieve some of my pain. Yet again, because he made me feel needed, I gave myself to him. Sun never just dropped me or stopped seeing me. Life just seemed to happen. We were walking on different roads. Even though our paths came together for a brief period, they parted and went their separate ways. So did we.

All I wanted, all I ever wanted, was for someone to love me. The sadness of who I had become told me I would have to seek, snatch, and hold onto the bits and pieces of the love I could get. Men had disappointed me. Now, it was my turn to repay the favor.

Five

I am My Fathers Daughter

Life as I knew it changed; I changed. Who was I? How had I gotten to this place? It had started with Devil Man and now I didn't know the person I saw in the mirror. I only existed, I functioned, I breathed, I walked, I talked, but I didn't know this person. Frequently I stopped and thought, "What's next?" My body responded, "Just breathe and survive, for tomorrow will bring about a day as empty as today and you have to survive it too, so just breathe." For what seemed like half a lifetime, I lived like this: just breathing and surviving.

Syrell and I still lived with my parents. I moved back in when I separated from my husband. I didn't feel like much in those days. My mom helped me to get through my divorce. She told me that if I could train myself to think about the good things my husband had taught me and not to focus on the divorce, then I would be able to find a way to go on and to not hate him. I tried to take her advice. I remembered how my husband had taught me that in life, no one will just give you a free pass. If you wanted something, you had to be willing to work for it. It reminded me that that was the reason I had gotten a job working as a bank teller. It was because he had instilled the drive to succeed in me. The goal gave me some peace, but my life would get worse before it got better.

My poor Syrell did not know what kind of mom he had. My parents told me years later how he had once said, "Grandpa, my mom don't love me." Hearing my dad say that made me cry. For I knew for all of those years of my being lost, Syrell had felt lost too. If Dad had told me his words back then, would I have tried to change? I would like to think so but probably not. At the time, I still could not think beyond myself. So, how would I have heard the innocent words of my little boy? Writing this book sure does make me sad. Thank goodness I have a forgiving son.

One night, I went with my girlfriends to a strip show. As usual, one of my family members had agreed to babysit Syrell.

I said to myself, "Let the party begin." It was exhilarating. The club was full of energy. As the strippers came out, I was sure they came straight from Ebony and GQ magazines. All I could see was muscle and beautiful shades of bronzy brown skin. I had never seen a stripper before, and the outfits these guys had on drove me crazy. The way they moved their bodies with such confidence made me want to imitate that boldness. The music they danced to was meant to bring out the beast in all the women at the club. Believe me, it worked.

One of the strippers, Carl, started to dance in front of me. My heart beat a lustful, desiring beat. I wanted him. For just a minute, I thought he wanted me as well. I started to dance with him. It seemed to get all the women excited, and the club went mad. The strippers danced. We partied and drank. There was a good time to be had, and we sure did have it.

We were still bursting with energy when the strippers finished. After they dressed and came out, they mingled with the women in the club. Carl, with a few of his friends, came over to our group and started talking. They expressed how encouraging it was to see our group get into their performance. We said it was our pleasure. Carl began a private conversation with me. He told me I was one of the most beautiful women he had ever seen. Wow, someone called me beautiful! He made me smile. He told me he wanted to take me out to get to know me better. I had no idea these pickup lines of deception had been used on many women. I felt so flattered and so needed by this stranger. His bronzy skin, his seductive lips, and his bulging muscles shouted freedom. I wanted some of it.

We left the club and had a late night breakfast. We talked about the joy of life and how much we all celebrated living it. No one asked why, if we enjoyed life so much, were we all still looking for happiness in someone else? In any case, we relished each other's company for several hours. As we walked out of the restaurant, Carl asked if he could take me out the following week. He always worked on the weekends but wanted to see me during the week. Of course, I said yes but told him I would meet him somewhere. After we agreed on a spot, he kissed my hand with his honey lips of deception as a goodbye.

All week I seemed to be on a high. The time breezed by. When the evening came for me to meet Carl, I could barely control myself. I hurried off after kissing my son goodbye. I told him he was going to have fun with his auntie. I barely noticed his sadness of spirit. I told myself he would have a good time because I wanted to believe it. How often I must have ignored his needs for my own.

Carl took me out to dinner. Over the meal, we laughed and talked. I felt like I had known him forever. He invited me to go back to his place. Without hesitation, I agreed. "But he's a stripper," I said to myself. The other part of me argued, "Shut up and roll with the punches." We were so excited; I left my car at the restaurant.

When we got to his place, he poured us drinks and put on soft music, and we sat on the sofa. He put his arms around me. The room started to spin with the excitement of what was to come. Nothing seemed to matter to me except that this man was about to take me. I wanted to see what this man who exuded perfection in body and in beauty would do to me. I felt like he could take me to places I only dreamed of.

He took me in his arms, kissing me with total passion. He caressed me with strength and desire. Time stood still. He took me to places I had only heard other women talk about. I felt so special. I thought we had just created something extraordinary. We lay in bed for a while, and then it was time for me to go home. As he drove me to my car, Carl said he would like to see me again. Smiling and excited, I agreed quickly.

It took a while for it to dawn on me that I had slept with a stranger on our first date. I did not even make him wait. No, just I gave my treasures away. Was my body a treasure to me? I decided it was not because I was of no value. I was all used up. Used goods... you can get them real cheap. My body, my possession, was used up. My body had never been pure or innocent, so why pretend? I told myself I couldn't help it. He seemed to love me. I know he desired me and I wanted to know what he had to offer me. I hoped that this was the beginning of a long, lasting relationship. How profound that this was what I found myself thinking in my mind!

I told my girlfriends about our evening. They encouraged me to take it all for what it was worth. Enjoy the trip and do not look back. So, I did. Carl and I continued to see each other every week or two. The passion remained strong, and each time excited me more than the previous.

One day, Carl came over, and he was upset. He had contracted a STD. It was my fault. He told me I needed to take myself to the clinic to get checked out and fixed. I was horrified because I had only been intimate with him during this time. The next day I went to the clinic to report that my boyfriend had a STD and requested that I be tested. After taking the necessary test, I found out I was clear. Once I had verification from the doctor, I called Carl immediately to give him the results. I told him I had been a fool to think that someone like him could be true. My negative test proved that he had been an unfaithful dog. I told him not to call me again and that he meant nothing to me. I thought that this was the end of him, but I was wrong.

Being a beauty in every way, Carl was used to running the show. He was the one who ended relationships and on his terms. My ending it was not going to work for him. He called me several times, but I refused to talk to him. One night I was at a show with some friends. Fortunately, we had backstage passes. When Carl came up to me, I ran from him and headed for the backstage area. When Carl tried to enter the restricted area, he was turned away. I thought he had gotten the message; but later in the evening, he caught up with me. He said he needed to talk to me and set the record straight. Ignoring how stressed out he seemed, I agreed to go outside with him. He asked me to sit in his car so we could talk. As he drove us to a remote place, I became more than a little concerned because no one knew where I was. I tried to tell myself that everything was going to be okay. Carl then took out a small gun. He told me I had shamed him and that he did not have much to live for. I knew if you take away a man's pride and self-esteem, they would do anything to prove they were a man.

I saw he was serious, and I went into survival mode. He told me he wanted us to get back together, and he did not know what would happen if we did not. I told him I loved him and wanted the same thing, but I had thought he did not want me anymore. He asked me to kiss him, so I did. When he told me he wanted to have me right there in the car, out of fear for my life, I let him rape me. "Would death be better?" I asked myself. My heart answered, "Who would look out for your son? Who would love and protect him? No, I must live. Tomorrow is a new day and somehow I will survive this." He drove me back to my car, kissed me goodnight, and left. My heart was beating out of control, and I fell apart. I was so grateful to be alive. I vowed I would never see him again.

A few days later, I drove over to one of Carl's friend's apartment. Red, another stripper, had always been kind to me. I wanted to talk to someone about what had happened. I felt so taken advantage of by Carl. I needed to find some reason for his actions. Who better to tell me than someone who danced with him? When I got there, Red offered me something to drink. He could tell I was disturbed and asked what was going on. I told him about the situation with Carl. He told me Carl's actions were unacceptable, and he would watch over me. I had nothing more to worry about.

His own chivalry must have excited Red because he began kissing me and telling me he would take good care of me. He said he had always wanted to be with me. He was the man that I needed. I didn't fight him. I had no more fight left in me, and he did say he would protect me. It was over almost as quickly as it had begun. As I put my clothes back on, I told myself that this was not the world I wanted to be a part of. When I walked out the door and closed it behind me, I decided to close that part of my life as well. As I drove home I asked myself, "Why did he feel a need to have me? Am I just a piece of meat to men? Why do they all seem to only want to have their way with me and then go the other way?" I decided men must know I was easy prey. I did not know how to change this, and I questioned if I even wanted to.

Since Carl had never been to my parents, he had no idea where I lived. I decided to not go out for a few months because I could not take the chance of running into him. When he called, I talked as little as possible but never agreed to see him. I always had something to do. He called less and less. Finally, he stopped.

I decided I needed to learn the game better if I was to survive in this world. The incident with Carl hardened my heart even more. The only thing that mattered was to not get hurt at all. I had a love/hate need for men. I needed them to make me feel beautiful and good. It was all that mattered.

I dated lots of men afterwards. You would think I would have learned from these two catastrophes, but my desire overcame my logic. I could not do without having men in my life. What kind of person was I? I hated how I felt at the end of each breakup, but I quickly found myself looking for the next relationship.

My next relationship was with Rich. He had been born and raised in Texas. I met him at the club. After dating a few weeks, he moved in with me. I should have known something was wrong when he didn't have a car, but he said all the right words and I let myself believe them. The trouble started within a few weeks after he moved in. He would borrow my car and be gone into the wee hours of the night. After the third time, I decided I needed so much more than what he was giving me. I ended the relationship. I packed his clothes and told him he had to leave. He called his brother to pick him up. It was over.

At the end of this quick relationship, I felt like a worm beneath the earth. I needed to find inner fulfillment. I needed something to take away that emptiness I had inside. I immediately started looking for my next dose of medicin; I needed another man.

Six

He Is Someone Else's Husband

There were certain things I had promised myself I would never do — no drinking, no drugs, no dating more than one man at a time, and no committing adultery. Liars lie to themselves. I had stepped into the dark side long before I realized I could not see. I was an adulteress in my heart with my first love but I categorized that as revenge. With my husband, I categorized the situation as karmic payback. I did not recognize myself as *that* girl until I was on my own and living in my own place.

I moved out of my parents' home and took my son with me. We moved into some apartments in Columbia. I enrolled Syrell in a Catholic school a few miles away from home. He was now about seven or eight years old. I began spending a little more time with him. During the week, we spent a lot of time together. Syrell seemed to be a much happier child when we moved into our own place. I went out only on the weekends I could get my parents or siblings to take care of my son. I entrusted Syrell to only family, and his godmother Rosa. I never forgot how easy it could be for someone to hurt him. One of the only things I did right during those lost days was to protect Syrell. I loved him in my own way with all of my heart.

Soon, I launched a relationship with a doctor. When I found out very early in the relationship that he was married, it did not matter. Other women had come in the middle of my relationships without a care in the world for me, so why would I give his wife a thought? The commitment they believed they had did not come from my mouth.

When I started dating this doctor, I was excited and super happy. We did not go out much due to his position, but we did spend time together. All too soon, he showed his true colors. He wanted a perfect woman, one he did not have to care for. He wanted an independent woman who could take care of herself. He wanted all the benefits of a relationship with none of the financial responsibilities of a caring relationship. This was a married man, one who committed himself to his wife, and he was busy sleeping with me. What planet was I living on? How could I even think that he was worth my time? Somewhere deep in my heart, I knew that if a married man cheated on his spouse, he would cheat on me as well. The newness always fades in these types of relationships. When it did, so did I.

One day I met a smooth-talking glass of poison. He put the Q in GQ. He was sure of himself, successful, and hands-down handsome. I should have known that a package wrapped that pretty was just a cheap remake of a real man on the inside. He knew all the right words to say and had a great sense of humor. When we were together, he gave me all of his attention. We played the game of good girl /good boy for a few weeks before I showed him the true me. I went to his office and loved him there. When he was feeling bold and his wife was out of town, I went to his house. I was grown and no one would tell me how to live again. I did not give any thought to how I would feel if some woman came to my house and slept in my bed. I actually thought this guy would leave his wife for me. Now, imagine trusting a man, who would invite me into his wife's bed, not to invite other women into my bed. Fantasy, please meet reality. It would only be a matter of time before he treated me the same way he was treating his wife. When his wife finally found out, I decided I was a lover, not a fighter. Before the going got rough, I got going.

My men went from bad to worse. Before I met Wren, I never cared for dark chocolate men. After meeting Wren, I thought maybe dark chocolate tasted, acted, and treated their women better. He had a southern charm that won me over. When we went out, he opened the car door for me. He treated all my girlfriends kindly. He did the things all women enjoy. He slowly began to win me over. When I gave myself to him, I thought, "This could be it. I can see myself with this guy." It felt so good, thinking that I might have finally found someone who cared about me. Should I let my guard down once again? I had to remember that no guy had added up to a true gentleman yet. Maybe there were no true gentlemen in the world. Maybe I would have to settle for half of a committed man. Maybe they only became true when they were old and washed up. Boy, I hated men. There were none who were good. But like a crackhead addicted to crack (the reason I say crack head is to illustrate how low I had allowed myself to go with men and how cheap I felt inside), I needed them to help me find the love I was looking for. I always found myself going back for more. More pain, more lies, more deceit, and, most of all, more broken-heartedness.

Wren lived a few states away. Because of the way he spoke, I believed him to be sincere. One day Wren told me he was in the process of closing on a new home. He wanted me to drive up to see the place and stay the weekend with him. What more could I ask for than a man who wanted me to share in his future? I dropped Syrell off at my parents, telling them some lie, and off I went. Things were great when I first got there. We looked at the landscape of his new home before going inside. A little later, another woman came over. I just felt awkward. My internal alarm, my inside gut feeling, told me something in the picture was not right. She seemed very sad. I could tell when she saw me she wanted to cry out. Wren told me he needed to talk to her and asked me to go inside to get ready for dinner. Wren left and did not come back until a few hours later. He told me she was an old friend of his, and she was going through a hard time. He needed to help her with a few things and that is what took him so long. I knew it wasn't true, but because he was so polite, I allowed myself to buy it.

The weekend went okay. I headed back home. On the way, I had to keep fighting that inner voice who told me this man was the worst. He must have put the "S" in snake. However, I was a woman who needed to believe in something, anything, so I allowed myself to believe the lies of Wren. A few months later,

Wren and I were talking on the phone, but something was off. It was like he was trying not to let the person in the room with him know that he was talking to his girlfriend. I tested my theory by telling him I was coming over the next evening for the weekend. He had no choice but to spit out a wonderous lie someone else might have swallowed. He said his old girlfriend had come over unexpectedly from Washington, DC. Her grandmother was terminally ill, and he did not have the heart to make her drive back such a long distance at night. Wren said she meant nothing to him, and she would leave early the next morning. He was sorry but I could not come over for the weekend because he had plans and would be away from home. The final light went on. He was a sour grape passing himself off as fine wine. I planned to do what all women do when rejected. I got even.

I called Wren's home when I figured he would not be home. I hoped this woman would be there alone. The phone rang twice when she picked up. I asked to speak to Wren and introduced myself as his girlfriend in South Carolina. I asked her who she was and she said Wren's girl also. "Are you the same woman who came over to his new house the week he moved in? Wren told me that you were an old friend he was helping to get over a few issues."

She said "No, I have been dating Wren for years."

Betrayal reared its ugly head, and I decided to put the nails in the coffin. I said, "I am so sorry to hear about your terminally ill grandmother. Wren said that's the only reason he let you stay the night. He said you were his old girlfriend, and he felt sorry for you and your situation; so he could not send you away in the middle of the night. I added that I had been to the house on several occasions and described the house with an intimately detailed description of the bedroom. When she told me she did not believe me, I told her I would drive up and we could confront Wren together. I told her I had nothing against her because she had not lied to me, but Wren had. I came off so sincere she knew I was telling her the truth.

She said, "No need to come up. I will be heading home as soon as Wren gets back in." Wren called the minute she finished reading him his rights. He tried to make everything my fault. I could tell that this was the woman he wanted to marry, but I hastened to tell him that one bad deed always deserved another. He said he had to drive her back to DC now. This was the whole story. He cared so much about her that he picked her up to spend time with him. I told him I was on my way over and that I would get to the bottom of who he was and whom he thought he was dealing with. I wasn't going anywhere close to him, but he did not know that. He told me he was leaving within the hour, and we would talk later. I believe I was always his back-up plan if things did not work out with his first choice. This thought became a reality when, two days later, Wren pulled up to my door. Acting as if nothing had happened, he thought that he could just walk back into my life. I showed him. I told him everything would be okay, but when he left, I never allowed myself to see him again. But, oh, did this harden my already hard heart! I cared about no one and no thing. I only knew I wanted to feel loved, and it did not matter from whom. I was getting totally tired of men and their issues.

I dated a nice guy, but it was never meant to go anywhere. He told me his parents did not believe in dating outside their race. He never wanted to get married or be heavily committed. I told him, "Then I am your girl, for I want nothing from you either except for the pleasure you can bring me." We dated for a while, but, as this relationship slowed down to a crawl, I found myself having problems looking in the mirror. Every time I gazed in the mirror, I did not know the person looking back at me. For a minute, it would scare me, but then I would tell myself to get over it and get on with it.

I started hanging out in the entertainment industry. Some partners and I were in negotiations with *USA Today* to provide an entertainment magazine insert. It was a great concept and seemed to have legs, but it never got off the ground. The possibility did grant us the opportunity to do many interviews with newly signed groups. I lived life in an even faster lane. I truly enjoyed the amount of attention I was getting. I did date my share of dudes, but every relationship ended as quickly as it had begun. After each, I found I had lost even more of myself.

One day I decided, it's done! I have had enough of men. There is none good, not even one. I set my heart on women, the same sex that believed as I did and liked the same things. I told myself we had so much in common I was sure other women were fed up with men as much as I was.

I remember saying to myself, "I seem to be attracted to both sexes." I found the curvature of a woman's body as beautiful as the carved-out design of a man's body. One day when I was picking up a friend to take her to work, I caught myself admiring her. I had always thought of her as a sophisticated young lady with lots of class. She carried herself in a self-assured way. She had a beautiful haircut that highlighted her face. I marveled at the way she would jerk it back. She was model thin and wore outfits that complimented her. I wanted so much to be a woman of class and to have that certain look about myself.

When I got to her house, she was in her bath towel. She let me in, but as she turned, the towel got caught on the door knob and fell off. I looked at her quickly and thought she had a beautiful body. I did not realize how that short appreciation would cause me to venture into a world that I should never have visited.

I set the attraction aside for many years because deep down I liked men. It was the way I knew I wanted to go. I knew I wanted more children and a husband could fulfill that desire. Plus, I liked the way I felt with men, but that did not stop me from sometimes wondering.

I toyed with the thought of being with another woman over

and over. I would allow myself to keep reliving the sight of this woman's body, and it excited me. I wanted to touch it, to taste it, and to feel it. I found myself wishing that I had made a move. At the time, I was in one of my many relationships, but the thought of another woman began to linger in my mind.

When I was at the end of my rope with men, I felt worn and torn by all of them. I decided that it was time to try something new. I came to the conclusion that there were no decent men left in the world. I believed the only reason they existed was to cause women harm.

One evening, a close friend I rarely got to spent time with, and I decided to go out clubbing together. We decided we would let our hair down completely. We wanted to be as free as birds. We would shake the hurts of the world off if only for one night. We had a few drinks, some drugs of choice, and decided we wanted to pick up a few men and take them back to my place. I had only tried cocaine a few times. She was the only person I ever did drugs with. I trusted her, and we looked out for each other. She wasn't like my other girlfriends I spent frequent time with; she was different, and I needed different. We selected two guys who seemed to want to spend some freaky time with us. We did not ask too many questions because we did not want to get to know them. We only wanted to know them for one night, nothing more.

When we got home, we had a few more drinks and laughed as we made small talk. One of the guys had too much to drink and fell asleep. I decided it was his loss. My friend had already taken the other young man into the bedroom and had started playing make-believe with him. I went into the bedroom where they were and she asked me to join them. I did not even have to think about it. I just got undressed and joined in the party. This is what I had always wanted to try. I am going to do everything and then some with these two. I realized she must have been curious too because quickly the party became all about the two of us. We blocked the guy out and went for each other. We did not care that someone was watching. We later included the young man. The three of us had a night filled with a new type of passion and desire.

In the early hours of the morning, the two young men left. My friend and I went to sleep. When I woke up, I asked myself, "Did this really happen?" As I turned in the bed, I woke up my girlfriend. I could not blame the alcohol and drugs anymore because they had worn off to some degree. It surprised me when she reached over and pulled me close to her. I gave in to my desire and we recreated the evening all over again. When our passion was spent, we showered; and she went home.

I replayed the event in my imagination and smiled. Weeks went by, but my friend and I could not bring ourselves to talk about what we had done together. Like with all other things that are not meant to be, this relationship ended before it had begun. Maybe I would give those men one more try.

Would Anyone Cry For Me?

Seven

Harder Than it Looks

When I looked in the mirror I hated who I saw. I could not even recognize the girl of my youth, maybe because there never had been a girl of my youth. Everything I had said I would not do, I did. I had never thought of myself as beautiful; in fact, I had never thought anything nice about myself at all. I felt sub-human and unseen by all, even by myself. Oh, I had fleeting happiness; but somehow, it always ended in pain and emptiness. I was complete when I was in the beginning and middle of my pleasure but dumbfounded when the pleasure turned to pain. Please believe me, it always did.

It took years for me to get to this point —the point of no return. I had lived life the way of the world but, even when I was doing so, I always remembered what my parents had taught me. I always knew there was another way. But to me, that way was too controlling, filled with what seemed to be no fun. That way told me what I could and could not do, and for almost all of my life, I ran from it. That way was really the way of pure happiness and joy, the thing I wanted most in life. But I had convinced myself that the cost was too great. Little did I know that the cost was free to me but had cost someone who cared more for me, more than I cared for myself, His life.

This is where so many of you will be tempted to close this book and think that it has nothing more for you. However, if you read it in its entirety it may change your life the way it changed mine. Not because it made me perfect as you will see, in the next chapters of this book. There will be continued honesty from me, and you will see how much I fought the old me to be the new me. What do you have to lose? We've made it together this far; let us make it to the end together.

One day in about 1994, when I wanted my life to be over, I did something I had not done in years, I prayed. I prayed to the God of my parents, the God of my first memory, and the God that could heal all of my deep, unresolved pain. I prayed and I pleaded with Him to change the girl I saw in the mirror. I told him I had to truly die to the person I saw, one way or the other. Either I would end the pain or He would. With everything in me, I knew I was at a crossroad. I was sad all the time, and nothing could take that sadness away anymore. No man, woman, or event could fill the void and emptiness I felt in my heart. Every time I tried to fill it, I felt emptier. I blamed myself for so much of the evil I had done to myself and to others.

"No greater love is there than the love of someone that would die for you." My parents raised me in the church, so I had heard those words before. At the time, the words had fallen on deaf ears. I believed in a God but not the Great I Am. I used to think that God just wanted to tell me what to do and how to live my life. He wanted to control me just to show that He could. I thought of the Bible as a book of dos and don'ts.

In saying all of this, you can tell I found myself sick and tired of always being at the tail end of my own life. How can I learn to love me? How can I change? This was my new dilemma; I wanted to, I needed to, but how? Syrell deserved better from me; and somewhere, I thought I could maybe be a better me. I knew I couldn't do it alone and I knew I needed to get rid of everything that was still holding the old me.

I was actually on my way to New York to break up with my entertainment attorney boyfriend when my new beginning started. I was at the airport when I was approached by a nice woman who was headed to NY as well. She introduced herself as Sandy and said she was headed to New York to visit some cousins. I found it easy to talk to her and told her why I was headed to the city. To my surprise, she told me that if things went wrong I could give her a call, and she would come get me. As weird as this sounded, I believed her. We exchanged phone numbers and spent the rest of the flight talking.

When I arrived in New York, my boyfriend picked me up. He took me to a nice hotel where his friends were waiting for us. We talked for a while before my boyfriend and I decided to go up to our room. We thought we would give it one last shot at trying to make our relationship work. It didn't. No intimacy or conversation could put something there that wasn't. We both decided that evening we were over.

Strangely, I didn't get too upset. I just called the airport and made reservations to fly home the following day. I decided not to call Sandy that day. After all, I had just met her and did not want to be a burden to her. I flew back home and decided I could see the writing on the wall for my life.

I called Sandy a few weeks later because I wanted to try to build a friendship with her. She invited me to go to church; and I said," yes." Early on Sunday morning, I found myself praying again to God. I told Him I was completely ready to change my life. I asked Him to help me make it happen. Syrell was about thirteen, and I was thirty-one when I decided we needed a new life. My biggest fear was that I had too many skeletons in my dark, secret closet. I thought, "How could a perfect God forgive an imperfect Betty?" I was resolved that I had no other alternative if I wanted to ever have a life. I needed to try to change me at any cost. We got dressed and headed to Sandy's church.

The church was located in Columbia, SC. When Syrell and I got to church, we felt warm and invited. There was a young teen ministry and Syrell got to spend time with other kids his age. I did not feel like everyone tried to read me like a book. I felt like this was a place of peace for me. The preacher preached about the forgiveness of God. He showed how Jesus had told a woman caught in the act of adultery that He did not condemn her but that she was to go and sin no more. I thought, "*Could it really be that easy?* Just ask for forgiveness and promise not to sin anymore? Then all my sins would be wiped away and I would be a new person? Wow, I'm in." I decided that day that I wanted to be a different person. The person I had been until that point just did not work for me anymore. I was all worn out. Like a tire showing its treads, ready to burst, and let all its air out, that was me. But could I? Did I have what it took to be different? I longed for a new me, but could I add up? I was so afraid because I had failed at everything I ever attempted, except having my wonderful son. Would I be accepted by these people who seemed to have life on straight? I felt so inadequate when I compared myself to everyone else in the room.

Sandy, seeing my fear and joy, whispered, "Are you enjoying the service?" I replied that I was but that everyone seemed to have their life on straight. She said, "You can, too. But, believe me when I say they don't have it on straight. They have learned how to depend on God when they are strong and when they have their struggles. Rome was not built in a day. Give yourself some leeway." Her words comforted me. I took a breath and relaxed.

Sandy, Syrell, and I started spending time together. I had lots of questions about God. She showed me how to research the answers for myself. Questions like: "Why does God allow innocent humans to get hurt? Does God expect us to be perfect? What if I had a relapse, would God disown me (Luke 22:33, 34; John 21:15-19)? Can you help me learn how to forgive (Matthew 6:14, 15; Romans 12:17-21)? How can God forgive me when I find it hard to forgive myself (2 Chronicles 7:14; Matthew 6:14)? How could I be sure that Jesus is truly the Son of God (John 1:1-18)? Do I have to believe and follow the whole Bible (Hebrews 4:12, 13; 1 Peter 2:21)? She had so much patience with me. Sandy treated me better than I treated myself.

I traveled with my new job as an inventory auditor, so it took me about three months to study and decide if I wanted to change my life. One day I was asked, "Do you want to get well? "I looked up in surprise. Then I asked, "What do you mean?"

"Well," Sandy replied, "you said that you were tired of the life you have led, but you have not decided if you want the new life you say you are seeking. So, I ask you again, do you want to get well?"

I thought about this question for a minute and then I said, "I want nothing more than to get well. I just have this fear of me! What if I'm not smart enough, strong enough, or hungry enough for the new me to stick with it? This is the thing that's holding me back... the fear of me."

Sandy smiled and said, "Girl, we all have had that fear, which means that you are on the right track."

Those were the words I needed to hear. I decided to wholeheartedly become a follower of God. I told myself I had given all I had to the old me, but now I would give all I had to the new me.

I realized that a person has to study to become a doctor. She does not just wake up one day and say, "I am a doctor." An Olympic athlete has to train for the gold prize. He doesn't just show up and expect to win. If I wanted to be a true Christian, I needed to use these same concepts. I started by studying. There were three things I had to decide. First, do I believe there is one God? Secondly, do I believe that Jesus is the Son of God? Finally, do I believe the whole Bible is the Word of God? The answer of my heart, was "YES!"

I had thought that by making this decision, everything else in my life would just fall into place. I would no longer struggle with the need to love and be loved. Man, was I wrong.

The first few months were easy because I was living on a high, knowing that I had decided to change my life. I attended church and all the functions they had. Syrell and I did things with other single parents and their children. He found a few good friends with whom he enjoyed spending time. Nevertheless, as the newness wore off I started to think about the old me and wondered if I had made the right decision.

The more I tried to do what was right, the more I wanted to return to my previous life. I took three steps forward and then one or two back. I longed for the touch of a man. Sometimes my heart said *any man*. The more I prayed for strength, the weaker I saw myself becoming.

When it first started happening, I told myself that if I pleasured myself I was not hurting anyone. This went on for months. The more I did it; however, the more I felt like a fake and loser. I prayed for strength and guidance but felt like I was leading myself down the wrong road.

My feelings came to a head. I needed a man, and I needed a man at all cost to me. Maybe I didn't want a man; I wanted fulfillment. In my weakness, I prayed, "Father, I am going to call one of my old boyfriends. If he answers the phone, I am going over to his home and give myself to him. Please don't let him answer. I do not have any self-control right now. I do not want to go back to my previous life, but I am picking up that phone. If he does not answer, I know You are saving me and You see me. Lord, I hope You see me. I know You will send me the strength and I will get beyond this weakness through Your strength. Ok, Father, I am picking up the phone to call. Who will answer?"

I was at a gas station, so I went to the pay phone. I picked it up, dialed the number, and it rang the first time. I said, "Please do not answer." It rang the second time. When it rang the third and fourth time, I said, "Thank You, Father, for hearing me. I am blinded by my own sinful desires, but I know You have bigger plans in store for me. I am Yours!"

This must have happened on a Tuesday because I was at a Bible study at church the next evening. When the preacher's wife saw me, she saw my downcast face. She came over, hugged me, and asked me how I was doing. I whispered that I needed to meet with her because I felt like I had fallen away from God. She saw my desperation and set up a time for us to meet the very next morning.

The next morning when we met, I told her about my masturbation and the need to be with a man. I continued with the prayer and phone call. I expected to hear a reprimand. Instead, I received encouragement. She said, "If you had fallen away, Satan would not be trying so hard to deceive you. It is when we are in the midst of our battle of good against evil that we feel our weakest. Those are the times when Satan puts all kinds of doubt in us to make us feel like we are not true Christians. No, you have not fallen away. Know that you are on the right road." Relief and joy jumped in my heart. I knew God was showing me the way.

She told me not everyone was meant to be single. Each of us had to make that decision for ourselves. Then she gave me great advice. She said, "If you want to find the husband who will be a blessing to you, make a list of everything you want in a husband. Then pray about it to God every day. Before you start, you must have faith that God will hear you and bless you with a husband." She encouraged me to remember that no one gets everything on her list but to trust that I would get the most important items. Something in me believed this advice. I decided to take it and apply it to my life. I met with the pastor's wife in late January, and I started praying as soon as I got my list together. On October 5, 1996, I got my answer.

Eight

Dreams Do Come True

Wow, I thought, there are only a few guys I could ever see myself being married to in our church. "God, I know you will have to work out a miracle."

I saw Isiah in church for the first time in November, 1995. I remembered one of the sisters saying to a few of us, "He's a little short, kind of good-looking, but wow, he can sing!" At this, I looked up at Isiah and said, "He is kind of handsome."

Little did I know he would be the man that little girls dream of!

Isiah was a divorced, young man who had just moved from New York with his teenage daughter, Tai. His skin was brown, and so were his eyes. He was 5 "5" and kind on the eyes. His voice resonated with warmth and hope. When he sang, he sounded like an angel. His singing made the hairs on my arm stand up.

I loved singing and thought I could hold a tune, so I joined the choir. One day at rehearsal, Isiah came in. His presence lit up the room because everyone loved hearing him sing. I could tell he was special, but how special I had no idea. I saw him several times during December, 1995, and February, 1996. Everyone seemed to be drawn to him. He was kind to everyone and treated them with love and respect. He was an Army man. His good manners stood out. It was more than just his singing; Isiah was genuine.

In March, something happened. Isiah asked if we could exchange children for a weekend every now and then. He explained that his daughter needed a mother. Her mom lived several states away in Virginia and she did not get to spend much time with her. Isiah did not want her to pick up only male traits from him. He offered to mentor my son. I could see how loving and kind he was to Tai and knew he strived to be a great single dad. He also had a younger daughter, Shameka. She lived with her mom. He had been unable to get custody of her when he got custody of Tai. She had been too young to tell the courts what she desired. His offer blew me away.

I had been praying about a husband for a few months. What I had been praying for was at least a 6-foot ymmm and Isiah was a 5-foot hmmm. I didn't realize that he was just the right size for me. We decided that the following weekend would work for both of us to exchange children. The plans were made. I found out Isiah's ex-wife had been unfaithful and decided she no longer wanted to be married to him. Isiah believed in marriage and had wanted to make it work at all cost. His ex-decided she wanted her freedom more. I realized that if he had that type of dedication to a woman who did not value him, how much more dedication would he have to a woman who did. Most of all, Isiah reminded me of my dad. Ymmm, could this be the start of something new! As my mother always said, "Time will tell."

Early Saturday morning, Isiah drove Tai, his fifteen-year-old, over and dropped her off with me. He picked up Syrell. The plan was for the teenagers to spend the night at the other's house and we would meet up at church the next morning. I was able to trust Isiah with Syrell for two reasons. First, Syrell was now a fourteen-year-old teenager, and through the years, I had had him repeat over and over, "Moms always protect their children." Secondly, Isiah was a godly man. I had been studying his character for a few months, and he was a man who practiced what he preached. I talked to other women and men at the church, and they all said the same great things about him. He was a man of value.

Tai and I went girly shopping and had dinner. We had a great time. I found out later that Tai opened up to me because I was the opposite of her dad's type. She knew her dad wanted a physically fit Barbie doll, but I was just the opposite of that. I was what I call "a real woman." I had nice-sized curves and a funny personality. I acted confident on the outside but struggled with my own weight issues on the inside.

Tai and I became friends. We spent a lot of weekends together doing girly things. I felt it an honor to mentor her and to be a part of her life. As time went on, we developed a bond. This bond would hold us through many days of discontentment with each other in the future.

Something else was happening as well. I started developing strong feelings for Isiah. We had been spending time together with our children, and it just started to feel right.

I often spent time with a girlfriend who had AIDS. I would have her over and help care for her. The bad thing about AIDS in the 90's was the fear it put in people's hearts. No one wanted to touch or get too close to someone who was infected. I felt the opposite. From studying the Bible, I knew that one of the most important things Jesus did for the sick was to touch them. I wanted to have the same kind of faith and love for others, so I made it a point to physically touch as many people as I could.

The turn of events was somehow unexpected. My friend and I ran in the same circle. We wanted to have fun and did not count the cost to our bodies or our health in doing so. My friend had hooked up with a "Down-Low" man. That is a man who was gay but did not want anyone to know so he dated and slept with women as a front. It was a way to have a career and keep up appearances. He was so lowdown he did not even tell her he was infected with the virus. She found out when she started getting sick. There still is no cure.

One evening, when Isiah and I were supposed to go to a single parent's event, my friend died. I asked him if we could go and spend time with her family instead. Being the kind man he was, he politely agreed. When we got to the family's home, I tried to encourage the women, and Isiah tried to support the men. Unknown to me, my friend's brother told Isiah what I had done for his sister. He told Isiah how much I had helped her. I had even helped to bathe her when she could no longer do it herself. He said their family was so grateful that God had put me in her life.

On the way home, I was emotional. With tears in my eyes, I thanked Isiah for going with me and told him how much it meant to me. He was very kind and told me he was glad that he had gone with me. Something sounded a little different in his voice. Was God working a miracle in Isiah's heart? He later told me after we got engaged that going with me to pay respects to my friend's family was the start of his caring for me as a woman. He later said after talking to her brother and seeing how kind I had been, it showed him my inner beautiful heart. Somewhere in his heart, he thought he could see himself with me for a lifetime. First, however, he had his own issues to deal with.

Isiah had a reputation for being a gentleman's gentleman on dates. I saw how true this was. Not only did Isiah open my door both going and coming from my friend's home, but he also made sure that I was okay while we were there. I could see why so many of the single women thought he was the best. After that night, something in me was beginning to think and feel the same way as well.

Isiah lived an hour away in another city, but we talked on the phone a lot. We talked about our children and what we wanted in our future. One day, Isiah suggested that we start praying together before we got off the phone. I thought, *"What a man. What a man!"* When we started praying together, our friendship grew.

I think Isiah could sense that I had feelings for him because of the boldness he began displaying. After listening to Isiah, I found myself saying to him, "Men are always looking for Barbie dolls. They think the grass looks so much greener on the other side, but if a man will water and nurture the grass he already has, it will be just as green."

Isiah said with confidence, "I know when a woman likes me!"

Knowing that he was talking about me, I told him, "When I like you, I will let you know. That way you do not have to guess." For some reason, it did not seem to go over too well!

A few weeks later, I felt myself feeling funny whenever I was around Isiah. I have a good friend who is married. She is wise, so I told her what I was feeling and asked for advice. She gave me a scripture to read to Isiah and told me to tell him how I felt about him. I prayed about it and decided to take the good advice.

When I called Isiah, I felt like my heart would beat right out of my chest. Somehow I mustered up the strength and courage to go through with my plan. The scripture I read said, "Better open rebuke then hidden love. Wounds from a friend can be trusted, but an enemy multiplies kisses," Proverbs 27:5-6. When I finished reading it, I said, "I read that to say I like you and I want to know if you like me, too!"

I could tell Isiah was caught off guard. He said he needed a little time before he could give me an answer. I waited three days for him to come back to say that he did not feel the same way.

To my own surprise, I said, "Okay, then let's work on the friendship," and that is what we did.

We continued to talk and pray together. We spent time with the children. About a month later, a neighbor was having a party; and I was helping her prepare for it. I did not want to go without a date, so I asked Isiah if he would escort me. He said he would be happy to. With his answer, it dawned on me that I really, really liked this guy. In fact, I loved him.

One Sunday after church, Isiah told me he was going to Virginia to drop Tai off for a visit with her mom for two weeks. He told me that he would be bringing his younger daughter Shameka back when he picked Tai up. He said Syrell and I would get a chance to meet and spend time with her. This made me very happy. I had spoken to Shameka once or twice on the phone; and now, Isiah wanted her to meet us. Because he was driving back alone, I suggested he take Syrell. Isiah thought it was a great idea. When they got to their destination, Tai's mom immediately asked who Syrell was. She said Isiah must like his mom. Isiah told her he was Syrell's "Big Brother," a father figure. Syrell's mom had thought it would be a help to keep him company on the long trip back home. Tai's mom said, "No, there is more to it than that."

When Isiah got back home to drop off Syrell, he told me about the conversation with Tai's mom. I knew she could sense that I cared for him. By his reaction, he must have shown he cared for me, too! We began opening up to each other and our unsaid feelings started to blossom. During the two weeks Tai was gone, we realized we really liked each other. Everything happened after the party that Isiah escorted me to.

Would Anyone Cry For Me?

Nine

Betty Has a Boyfriend, a Best Friend

A week before the girls came home, Isiah promised to escort me to a party at my friend B's home. The day of the party, I was busy helping my friend prepare. About an hour before the guests were to come, I told her I needed to go home, shower, and change. She asked me if I would run to the store around the corner and pick up a few last minute things for her before I returned. Wanting to be helpful, I agreed.

It was a very hot day. In the privacy of a home, I had on very short shorts. Their length, or lack of length thereof, did not dawn on me until I went to the store on my way home. I was in line after picking up the ice cream when I saw Isiah. He was looking at me and I could sense him saying," Wow." (Okay, he told me this part later.) I felt my heart racing. Suddenly, I felt the shortness of my short pants.

Isiah came over to greet me. I could see him staring up in the air. I said, "Do not look down. I have on inappropriate shorts; and if you look, you will not like me anymore." I began to panic. I quickly explained I was just doing a few last minute things for the party before I got changed. I had been over at B's house helping her all day. I thought no one would see me. When she asked me to pick up a few items, I had stopped by the store, which was on my way home.

I asked Isiah why he was at the store. It was still very early for the party and the store was only two minutes from my house. Then I saw he had flowers in his hand, which he was trying to conceal behind his back. Knowing I could see them, he said, "These are for you." As we paid for our items and were leaving the store, I asked Isiah to walk in front of me. He did and began to laugh. I thought it was at me, but truly, it was at the situation.

I told Isiah I was going home to shower and change. He said he would come over in about 30 minutes to take me to the party. I got in the car and started praying about what had just happened. I asked God to help Isiah see that what I had said was true and how I had thought I was in a safe place at B's house.

We went to the party, but I could tell Isiah was a little uneasy. He acted a little nervous, which was completely out of character for him. He was always the guy everyone wanted to be around and talk to, but that night, he was a little distant. When we left the party, he dropped me off at home and said he would talk to me later. Being me, I said, "But we haven't prayed together yet, and we always pray before you leave." So, we sat in his car and prayed. He said a few words that I was able to piece together, and I realized what he was trying to say. He said things such as, "I do not want to stop you from going to college,"

My reply, "They have colleges all over the state."

Then he said, "I do not want to stop you from seeking your dreams."

My reply, "God gives the fulfillment of dreams in many different ways."

Then he said the words I had been waiting to hear. He said, "I like you." The next thing I write is true, true, true. We started making plans to get married and spend the rest of our lives together right then and there! It was at that very moment in time that we both decided in our hearts that we wanted to spend the rest of our lives together. Even though we were not officially going steady, we knew we wanted to get married. Isiah hadn't even said the words, "I love you," yet we were making plans. Time stood still. We knew we each had found our soul-mate. I felt more like a fifteen-year-old teenager than a thirty-two-year-old woman. I thanked God for the miracle I saw unfolding before us.

We knew we wanted to keep ourselves pure for our wedding night, so Isiah walked me to the door and bade me goodnight. I went in the house so excited. When I told my roommates Isiah and I were going to get married, they told me to slow down because we were not even steady dating yet. "I know, but we are going to get married-and soon."

Tai finished her few weeks with her mom. The time came for Isiah to drive to pick up the girls. Instead of driving all the way, his ex-decided she would meet him halfway. When he picked up the girls, he was so happy. He loves spending time with his baby girl and relished every minute of it. He brought the girls over to see Syrell and me.

Shameka was a doll, innocent as a six year old should be. She gave me a hug. We loved each other from the beginning. We all spent the weekend having fun.

Soon, it was time for Tai to go on her trip to Romania. The three of them came over; and we took Tai shopping for the things she needed for the trip. The five of us had a great time. We arranged for Tai to get her hair done by Rosa, Syrell's godmom. When we dropped her off, we told her we would see her in a few hours. As we came to pick her up, she was happy and giddy. She told us her mom wanted all of them to go on a family trip with her. Without stopping to think, I said, "Oh, where are we going? Because I know you guys are not going on a family trip without me." I could tell this burned Tai to the bone. She felt like I was invading their space. I knew her mom was trying a last ditch effort to win Isiah over even though she had wanted nothing to do with him for years.

Isiah, being a man who believed in family, had tried on several occasions to reunite with his ex-wife. She had told him she wanted no more to do with him and she was going on with her life. As time went on, Isiah decided it was time for him to go on with his life as well. He believed God would give him a wife that he could love and devote himself to.

Knowing how women sometimes think, I knew what the ex was up to. I became like a wild animal protecting her mate. I knew I could not let it happen. I knew Isiah and I wanted a future together. I couldn't let Tai's mom get in the middle of our relationship. I knew I had to protect my man.

With much confidence and resolve, Isiah agreed with me and told Tai that if they were to go on a trip, Syrell and I would go with them. You could feel the tension in the air. Tai was as hurt as a teenager would be who wanted her family together. She must have relayed this to her mother because we heard nothing more about a family trip.

A week before Isiah and I had the conversation about our feelings, I had planned a trip to Virginia. At the time I planned the trip, I was looking at a possible move. I did not know where Isiah's heart was, and I wanted to get away from any possible future hurts. I thought it would only be a matter of time before he decided he did not want to be friends anymore.

I told Isiah about the trip and how I could not cancel my plans because my cousin would be hurt. He wished me a happy, safe trip and said he would call me every night. On the third night, Isiah said to me, "Betty, over the last three days I realized something, 'I love you.'"

Can I say my heart skipped a beat? If I could have, I would have gone back home that evening. Then he sang me our special song, "A Whole New World." "I can give you the world, shining, shimmering, splendid, now tell me, Betty, when did you last let your heart decide? I can open your eyes. I'll take you wonder by wonder, over, sideways, and under on our magic carpet ride. A whole new world, a new fresh start it's going to be, no one can tell us no or where to go or say we are only dreaming." He told me we would make definite plans for our future together when I got back home.

A few days later, I returned home. That weekend, Isiah came over. We talked about the kids first. He said he had promised Tai that he would talk to her before he asked any woman to be his girlfriend. Tai was due back from Romania the next weekend. I told him I completely understood and that I would speak to Syrell as well.

Weeks before this happened, I had given my cousin the okay to have her 50th birthday party at my home. This would be the same weekend Tai was due home. On the day of the party I was focused on helping my cousin prepare. I had no idea how Isiah would handle the situation with Tai. With so many people in the house, I knew that it would be difficult to give her the privacy she would need. Isiah said not to worry, because he had a plan. Here is what happened. We knew we did not want to tell Tai about our newfound love before her missions trip to Romania. We decided to wait until after she got home. We knew, it might devastate her. We did not want her depressed while far from home in a foreign country.

Isiah picked Tai up from the airport and came straight over to the house. The party was already in full swing when they arrived. I was helping in the kitchen. Isiah came out back to ask if he could make an announcement and sing a song. Of course we said yes. He approached me, took my hand, and, in front of everyone, asked me if I would be his girlfriend. "Yes! Yes!" I exclaimed with a smile, joy, and tears. Then he sang, "You are so beautiful to me." Those words made me feel so special, and I was as happy as the birthday girl. I am even giggling now as I write this down. Unknown to me, he had already arranged this with my cousin.

I whispered to him, "Did you get a chance to talk to Tai first?" He said, "No worries, it is taken care of." I did not see Tai for a long time that evening. When I finally did, I saw her downcast eyes. I knew things had suddenly changed between us. Normally Tai would have come over, given me a hug, and told me all about her trip. Now, she seemed to keep her distance from me. I could tell she was not happy; but in my heart, I told myself that in time love would win her over.

I did not know until about ten years later what had happened. When she finally told me, I told her I would have "teenage hated" me as well. As she and Isiah had approached the house, Isiah said, "I like Betty; I am going to ask her to be my girlfriend, and I am going to ask her now!" There was no talking about it. He had decided what he wanted, and it was just a matter-of-fact statement he made to her.

Tai complained, "Dad, you told me you would talk to me first. You have given me no warning, no breathing time, nothing. How could you just announce that you are going to ask this woman to be your girlfriend and right now?" He did not let her say another word. He left her sitting bewildered on the step outside. We may all laugh about it now; but at the time, it was the end of the world for our daughter.

While Isiah and I knew we wanted to get married, we both agreed we needed to give the children several weeks to get used to the idea. We dated about six weeks when Isiah decided to have a talk with my dad. We went down to my parents' house and Isiah asked my dad if he could have a talk with him. My dad said, "Sure, let us go for a walk." Now Isiah had never been in the country, so he was unaware of all the insects that were out during the summer. As he walked with Dad, he found himself swatting insects. My dad, being a country boy all his life, just walked with his hands folded behind his back.

Isiah told my dad he loved me and wanted to marry me. He would protect me for the rest of our lives. Then he asked for my dad's permission.

My dad replied, "Yes, you can marry Betty, but you know you're getting my wildest child. Do you think you can handle her?"

Isiah laughed and said, "Of course, Sir. I love Betty. God will make a way." So happy he had gotten my dad's approval, Isiah and Dad came back to the house. We all visited a little while before Isiah and I left for the park downtown. Before we got there, we stopped at our favorite restaurant, Subway, and got our usual — the one-dollar deli sandwich. We were sitting down at the park eating when he saw me biting into the sandwich in which he had slipped my ring. Isiah got down on one knee and said, "Betty, of all the women in the world, my heart only beats for you. Will you marry me?"

I got goose bumps. I knew I would spend the rest of my life with this man. I told him "Yes! Yes! Yes!" He gave me a kiss on the cheek and a kiss on my hand. I knew I was his and he was mine.

Afterwards, we laughed, talked, and planned our future. Our thoughts shifted to our children. We knew the first thing we needed to do was to sit down with them and tell them we were going to be married. After we left the park, we picked them up and took them home; so we could tell them before we told anyone else.

Our children showed such different emotions. Our son, who was now fourteen, took Isiah aside and told him he was okay with us getting married, but Isiah had better not hurt his mom. Tai at sixteen, did not say much of anything. It was like she was in shock her dad wanted a life with me — really with any woman. This was understandable because she and her dad had been together alone for so long. She was used to being the woman of the house. The thought of sharing her dad was more than she could bear at the time. We assured our children God was in control, and we would become a true family. We asked them to give it time. Everything would fall into place.

Another situation which needed to be handled was with a sister at church. She really cared for Isiah. They spoke a lot on the phone. She had believed that one day he would ask her to marry him. When Isiah and I talked about it, I told him that before we could tell anyone else, he needed to talk to this sister to make sure she was okay. If the situation had been reversed, this is what I would have wanted. It would help me to get over him in all the right ways. Isiah called the sister and told her we were engaged. He wanted her to know before he announced it at church the next day. She told him how much she really appreciated his thoughtfulness in telling her first and that she was happy for him but a little sad for herself.

The next day, we went to church as a family. Isiah had arranged to have an announcement made about our engagement. We were asked to stand up when the announcement was made. The church applauded, but I noticed one girl crying and going downstairs. After we sat down, I told Isiah I needed to go and check on someone. I went downstairs, found the girl crying, and asked her what was wrong. She told me that she had thought she would be the one to marry Isiah. I told her how sorry I was about that. She said Isiah had been such a gentleman to her and so kind, and she wasn't used to that. Gently I told her Isiah was kind to all the women in church. He opened the door for all the women because he believed that as a brother he needed to treat them all as sisters. I told her I would pray God would send her a husband. I hugged her and went back upstairs.

When I got upstairs, Isiah asked me if everything was okay. I told him what had happened and asked him how many other sisters believed he would marry them. I told him we women were not used to a man treating us with such love and admiration. It would confuse any girl and make her think it was love.

After church, Isiah decided he would check on the sister to make sure she was okay. He told her he cared deeply for all the women at church. He wanted to make all of them feel special because they were special women. She smiled and told him she understood and congratulated him on our engagement.

Wow, in a year-and-a-half, I had gone from feeling lost to finding my soul-mate! I had been a girl without hope, but now I was a girl full of dreams for the future. I went from needing to be encouraged to encouraging others. I felt like the most blessed woman in the universe.

Ten

The Wedding

As single parents, Isiah and I did not have a lot financially. Our favorite restaurant was Subway. We learned together that happiness was much more important than having a big wallet. We knew that if we waited on our budget to grow, we would not be able to marry for years. We decided that by putting our two single families together, our bottom line would be covered each month. More importantly, we would have each other and our children. We looked at our budget and believed we only had about $1000 we could put towards the wedding. We were convinced that the only thing that mattered, when it was all said and done, was that we were one.

The good news was I would wear our family wedding dress. My sisters had married in it. My brother, Asa, would cater the affair. We would have a potluck at the rehearsal dinner. We accepted everyone's offer to help but told them we had no money. If they wanted to provide anything, they would have to do it voluntarily. When you are honest with people, they are really ready to help you. There was a couple getting married the weekend before us. We asked if we could use their decorations. They were so happy to oblige. My rings were Isiah's grandmother's. They had been given to him as family heirlooms. We bought Isiah's ring from the pawn shop. He loved it as if we had purchased it new. Our bridesmaids had their dresses made by a friend of the family and she charged very little to make them. The groomsmen rented their own tuxedos and we got our son's tuxedo free. A very close friend of the family directed the wedding. We just kept it simple.

My favorite and most memorable parts of the wedding were twofold. The first was my dad walking me down the aisle. I was so proud he was my dad. The second was Isiah singing me down the aisle. He sang *"One in a Million to Me."* It is still one of the happiest memories I have. My husband told me and the world I am his everything.

Isiah picked up Shameka a few days before the wedding.

Shameka was so happy to be with us again. She melted right in and accepted us as a family right away. Of our three children, she was the only one who seemed completely happy about our marriage. Tai and Syrell seemed to just be holding on. It was a huge hurdle for our two teenagers who knew the disappointments of their past and did not know what their future held. Shameka was thrilled to be a part of the wedding. We were excited she, her sister, and, now, her new brother were a part of what God was putting together.

We decided we wanted a brief reception. After the wedding, we had the traditional toast, cake cutting, and introductions. In lieu of gifts, we asked everyone to contribute to our wishing well. We knew this would help us more than gifts because we were combining two families. We skipped the music and the drinking because we knew that that would cause people to stay longer; we, however, wanted to get to our honeymoon.

Isiah and I had decided that we wanted to have a real honeymoon. We determined to do it God's way and not be intimate until our wedding night. This was so much harder than it sounds. It might sound like a walk in the park, but I think the body knows once you make a commitment to each other; it wants to take it all the way in a hurry.

I thought my friends and colleagues would compliment us on our decision to wait, but they didn't. They kept telling me what a fool I was to not "take the car for a ride before buying it." They also asked "who buys a cow without drinking some milk first?" They seemed so upset that Isiah and I had decided to wait until our wedding night to fully know each other. They put a lot of pressure on me to change my mind, but I held steadfast to the decision we had made. I knew that it was not always easy. A few months before we got married, Isiah and I decided that Syrell and I needed to move to his city. We wanted Syrell to start school and not have to change schools a few months into the year. We decided Syrell would go ahead and move in with Isiah, and I would live with a super nice woman whom I called Grandma Ella. I would go over and prepare meals for the family and spend time with them, but I would go home in the evening.

One day I had an insatiable appetite for Isiah's loving. We were all at the apartment. The kids were watching a movie. I told Isiah I needed to speak to him in the kitchen. He had a walk-in pantry. I took him in the pantry and quickly pulled up my shirt. I told him I wanted him to just touch me. I know he saw the desperation on my face. He gently told me to pull down my shirt and reminded me we were going to wait for our honeymoon. He told me we would have the rest of our lives to express our love and that it would be worth the wait. I pulled my shirt down in dismay but thought, "This man really loves me!"

Man, am I glad he held steadfast to the decision and commitment we had made to God. When I was weak, he was strong! I believe his strength is a big part of why we are so close today.

Our honeymoon was amazing. I told Isiah before we became one that I wanted us to pray and thank God for putting us together. The one desire I wanted more than anything else was to start our honeymoon and new life together with God being first. Isiah agreed and said he wanted us to pray first as well. When we got to the room, we stopped, held hands, got on our knees, and thanked God for each other. Isiah prayed and I saw in him what real dreams are made of. I knew, without a doubt, that God had opened His treasure box and given me one of his most valuable gifts, Isiah!

For the very first time, I felt like a virgin. Isiah took me in his arms and kissed away all my sadness. All I could feel was his love for me. It was so right. I was so happy because Isiah swept away all the despair in me and filled all of my past pain with happiness.

We had no money, but I felt rich. We rented an apartment, but Isiah made it a home. We had everything. We had our children and each other.

When we returned from our honeymoon, the hard work of marriage began. We needed to build the five of us into a family. We knew we would be getting Shameka a few times a year. We wanted to make sure she felt as special as our children who lived with us full time. How difficult the task would be, but we didn't care because we knew anything worth having was worth working for. We decided we would focus only on each other for the first few days of our honeymoon, and we did. Then, we decided we needed to talk about how we were going to meld into a family.

Would Anyone Cry For Me?

Eleven

The Two Families Become One

We wanted to set our household up for success. Because our children were teens, we decided that Isiah would enforce the hard discipline with Tai, and I would do the same with Syrell. The two of them had been alone with each parent all their lives. It was only natural that each child would forgive his biological parent for the discipline but would hold a grudge against the new parent. Shameka was only eight and lived with her mom. Because she was so young, we decided that we would work with her together.

Our children stayed with our best friends while we were on honeymoon. When we picked them up, we began the work to make our family one unit. Our son was easy because he just wanted his mom to be happy, but our daughter was a major work in progress. It wasn't all Tai's fault. Her mom was meddling, feeding her all kinds of stuff that caused disruption in our family. I knew her mom's pain kept her mom from knowing how much she was hurting her daughter.

She kept telling Tai how she wanted her family back. This made it hard for Tai to feel that we were her family. There was such division in her heart. One day I picked up the phone while they were talking. Her mom was crying. I told Tai to let me speak with her. Tai's mom told me that everything she and Isiah had dreamed of he now shared with me. As kindly, lovingly, and gently as I could, I told her I understood where she was coming from. I told her I would pray for God to bless her with a husband, but she could not have mine. After we got off the phone, I didn't know what to do, but I did the only thing that made sense to me. I prayed for her to be happy.

We told our children that God gives people two kinds of children, biological babies and children parents love completely by choice. We told them they were our children, and we couldn't love them anymore even if they had come from our bodies. We also told them that they never had to choose which parents to love because there was room in their hearts to love all of us.

We never referred to them as stepchildren or half-brother and sisters, for this would mean that they were not fully a part of the family. Think about what do you do with the step? You put it under your feet; you stand on it; dirt gathers there and you think of it as filthy. Besides, what is a half? It means that it's incomplete not whole; our children were not this for us. We taught them they had two moms and two dads who loved them completely. Who came up with these two words, "step and half," anyway to describe a loved one?

If the world started treating combined families this way, how many more children would feel like a complete part of the family? I believe this would enable them to be the happy children we all want. If parents did not say negative things about the other parent in front of the children and would allow the children to love each parent, how much healthier the children would be! Children were never meant to carry the burden of their parents' broken hearts. Children love both their parents. When put in the middle of their hatred for each other, the folks who get destroyed are usually the children. When a person is hurting, they will do almost anything to relieve that pain. If an ex-spouse is the source of the pain, nothing will be spared to get even. Most times parents do not even know the heartaches they inflict on the children they love. This heartache can even lead to the self-destruction of the child.

Tai started to show her pain and heartache. She began to be very disrespectful to me. She treated me with contempt and hatred. I tried to be as patient as possible; but many times, I was nearly at a breaking point.

I questioned what I had gotten myself into. I voiced my concern to Isiah. Our household could not last if we did not figure out how to get the situation under control. Isiah decided he needed to have a talk with our daughter about what would and would not be tolerated. In a private conversation, he explained to her that he and I were married now and functioned as one. She responded that she had known him longer and better. How could he say that I was one with him? He consoled her by telling her that one day she would fall in love and the only thing that would matter to her was her husband. She would put her dad in the back of her mind and fill her mind with her new love. He told her that all children want all of their parents' attention until they start caring for their first love. He told her that his love for her had never changed and that the love a husband and wife have for each other is different from the love parents have for their children. He hugged her and told her that only when she discovered the love of a mate would she understand the difference.

Next, Isiah told Tai he could not allow her to disrespect me. If the blatant disrespect continued, she would have to go live with her mom. She was furious. She asked him how could he choose me over her, his daughter. He explained that he wanted both of us in his life and in our home, but we all needed to do our part to make the family work. She told her dad she did not know if she could or wanted to change. Isiah told her the choice would be hers as to what road she would choose. She knew what the outcome would be if she did not work on changing.

Tai, like most women, was rebellious. She decided to see if her dad would make good on his word. She began to disrespect not only me but her dad as well. When Isiah could not take it anymore, he pulled Tai aside and said he was sending her to live with her mom. He told her that if she did not want to be a part of the family, he would grant her wish. Tai, being a young woman, said, "I don't care. When am I leaving?" He told her it would be about a month before she left. The tension in the house grew. The only thing that kept me sane was knowing that it was going to end soon.

About a week before Tai was to move, she asked her dad if she could have a talk with him alone. I, being the controlling wife, sensed something was up. I wanted to be a part of the conversation, but Isiah told me he wanted to talk to her alone. They went outside to the car to talk. Tai acknowledged that she really did not want to leave. She wanted to stay with us and she would work hard toward being a part of the family. Isiah, loving her with all of his heart, agreed to her remaining with us.

When he came back in the house, Isiah explained that he had made the decision to let Tai stay with us. Can you say, "Betty was a mad woman?" I felt my body catch on fire. Lo and behold, this would be our first fight. I asked him how he could make a decision like that without talking to me first. When I asked him what rules he had laid down or what expectations would she have to meet, he said, "None, I just told her she could stay."

I said, "If she stays, then I leave." I worked a job which required me to leave home around 4:00AM, Monday through Thursday. I still worked as an inventory auditor and traveled all over the Southeast. I felt like I could not breathe but told Isiah I was headed to work. It was only about 1:30AM. Isiah did not want me to leave and called a couple who mentored us. He explained what had happened. Burt told him to ask me to speak to his wife. I replied, "Nope, you talk to her." Burt told him to ask me to pray. He told him that if I refused, Isiah should get on his knees and pray anyway, let me leave if I chose, and take one step at a time.

Isiah asked me to pray. I told him, "No way." I did not want to pray or have anything to do with him. I could see the hurt in his eyes, but I didn't care. Pain for pain is what I told myself. Isiah, realizing we could not fix the situation quickly, decided to go back to his foundation, God, and pray for guidance. As angry as I was, when I saw Isiah on his knees praying, I remembered the commitment I had made, first to God, then to Isiah. I got on my knees on the opposite side of the bed as my husband prayed. He cried out to God to help him be the husband and father he needed to be. Slowly I moved to the back of the bed. As Isiah continued to pray to God that he was only human and filled with mistakes, I found myself right beside him. I knew if he was praying to God about his shortcomings, then he was not focusing or pointing his finger at me. The prayer brought a peace into the room. Isiah and I decided to talk it through again. This time, we listened to each other's concerns.

Isiah loved Tai with all of his heart and didn't want to lose his daughter. He was committed to being there for her, if she let him. He believed he would be able to help guide and influence her life the way a daddy should. Hearing this reminded me that he was really a great dad, but my concern wasn't so much that she was going to stay with us; it was the fact that he had not talked to her about what was expected. Also, while this was true, a part of it was that in my heart, I was selfish and felt like she had gotten one over on me. This disrespectful teenager had gotten the last laugh. I knew I was supposed to be a Christian, yet I still had this thought. Was I fooling myself?

After work the next day, I met with a friend I respected. I told her what had happened and about the evil thoughts I was harboring. She told me that in order to give our family a real shot at being happy, I needed to decide what kind of mom I wanted to be. Did I want to be a mom who only loved my children when things were going well? Or, did I want to be a mom who nurtured and guided my children to success? She asked me if I had been the perfect child I expected Tai to be? *"Wow, that cuts to the heart!"* I, thought. I prayed and thought deeply about this conversation for days. I realized that if I were to put unrealistic expectations on Tai, I would never be able to help her become the wonderful woman I knew she could be. I remembered my mom and her unselfish love. I decided to be that mom as well.

It took us weeks of hard work to get over ourselves. We all started with baby steps. As we each did our part, we mended the relationship and started enjoying being a family. I do not want to give the impression that we did not have our growing pains. We did. We still had to learn to give and take in the right way, but we stuck with our commitment to love.

Ten years later, when Tai was about 25 years old, she called me one day to thank me for being her mom. She told me I had helped her to become the woman she is today. I must tell you, it made me feel so honored. I followed the example God gave me in my mom. I love my girls; and, in the end, love did not fail us.

The next big issue we had struggled through was spending quality and quantity time with our baby girl, Shameka. After we had made the arrangements to get her for the summer, her mom decided to shortcut our plans. She called Isiah to tell him the conditions he had to meet in order to get Shameka. The new plans were the opposite of what we had planned. She knew Isiah would agree to almost anything to spend time with our daughter. The switch would have been bad enough, but she decided that she must be the one to call me and inform me of what she and my husband had just decided. I could not let her know that her actions cut me to the core. I simply said, "Thanks, but I will talk to Isiah myself about any change of plans." I got off the phone quickly and started to cry. Didn't Isiah know what he had just done to me? Of course, he didn't know, but I would make sure this would not happen again.

The minute Isiah got home, I confronted him. I told him that in Shameka's mom's eyes, he cared more for her than me because she had made him change our plans. He told me I was being jealous and blowing things out of proportion. I realized I was doing just what she had hoped I would. I was pushing Isiah away. I stopped dead in my tracks and asked Isiah if we could pray about the issue to get it resolved. We prayed. God opened our eyes to the fact that He had joined us together. We decided not to let anyone else get in between us again. Isiah would talk to me first before he changed any decision we had made. Isiah decided, from then on, that I would be the one who would communicate with his ex about any plans for our children. He said setting up our children to win was the most important thing. I could trust him to lead our family. This was one of our last big fights. Only a year-and-a-half into our marriage, we realized we were finally beginning to get it all together. I had thought that because we loved each other, we were supposed to be problem free from day one. I quickly realized that that only worked in the movies. In reality, you get out of your marriage the work you put into it. We grasped the concept that he was a man and I was a woman. We thought differently. We realized, in order to make good decisions for our home, we would always have to discuss the way to handle situations. We also knew that someone had to have the final say so. Wanting to follow the Bible, I told Isiah that he was the man and the leader of our family. I promised him that he would have the last say if we could not come up with a solution together. In addition, I promised him I would never say, "I told you so." This was truly what I felt in my heart. I just had to train myself to live it.

Our decision on discipline became important a few years later with Syrell. He had gotten his driver's license and was on our insurance. Each morning, he would drive himself and Tai to school. They were well pleased with their new freedom. When Syrell got his license, we told him we would carry him on our insurance, but if he got a ticket or was in an accident because of negligence on his part, we would take his license for six months. When he resumed driving, he would have to pay his own insurance. Tai was a witness to the conversation. We had him repeat to us the agreement to ensure he understood. He did. Several months into the school year, Syrell was on his way to school. Traffic was backed up and, instead of waiting to see what the problem was, Syrell decided to speed around the car. In his haste, he hit a parked car. When we got home from work, we saw the car had been in an accident. We looked the car over before going into the house. Tai and Syrell told us what had happened. We first inquired if the kids were okay. They both said they were fine. We started laughing, saying the car got the worse end of the stick.

We told Syrell we needed to speak with him in his room. Privately, we asked him to repeat what we had agreed would happen if he got into an accident. He did and I reached out my hand for his driver's license. With total dismay, he handed his license to me.

Taking his license was only the first part of the ordeal. The second affected the whole family. Now, we had to take the kids to school before we went to work. Tai came home frustrated and asked why she had to suffer because of Syrell. We explained that when the going was good, she enjoyed the benefits. When the going got rough, she would have to adapt to that situation also.

We knew that if Isiah had inflicted this punishment, Syrell might not have forgiven him. While the episode is now one of our very funny, family memories, it wasn't funny when it happened. Thankfully, time puts all things into perspective.

Please know our marriage is no fantasy. For Isiah and me, no matter how much we gel together, we always have a thorn in our side. Isiah was a military man. He believed in being physically fit. I grew up with physical fitness not being a part of my daily routine. I felt like Isiah was trying to control me and mold me into his own little Barbie doll. I was not having any of it. He seemed to always talk about what I ate and would tell me when I had had enough. At first, I brushed it off. I just dealt with it. Then it became more than I could bear, and we would have a discussion. We had in our corner a good thing; we were always able to meet with a couple from the church and talk it through. No matter how great things would be going, every year or two my weight became an issue. Even today, we find that this is still a problem. The difference now is how we handle it. I mention this because everyone should know that no matter how happy two people are, they will never agree on everything. The key is to figure out how to live with having a difference of opinion.

For me I had to ask myself if I loved being unhealthy and at the weight I was. My answer to myself was, no. But no matter what I did, success was not to be mine. Then one day as I was writing this book, I started to pray to God for the control I needed to beat my body into shape. To be at a weight that I liked and to find some kind of enjoyment in working out. The Spirit in me whispered to my soul, "I believe in you and I know you can do it," and ever since then I have been striving to stay on the right track.

Why am I writing all of this down and putting it out there in cyber space? Is it because I want everyone to see how weak I still am, how I fight to do what is right, how I still make bad decisions? YES, it is all of the above.

You see, if you expect a perfect life, then you will always be disappointed. If you expect others to change you and make you happy, you will be left waiting. However, if you strive to understand life and see that all of us are the same inside, well then you will hold the key to your life being complete and successful. Once you have decided what success is for you, then do not let anyone make you feel unseen and unspecial.

Twelve

Persevering through Tragedy

What a world of difference my life is today! I thought no one could be this happy and fulfilled. I kept expecting to wake up and find my world shattered. One day, it did.

Isiah had retired from the military, and we had moved back to South Carolina. After several months had passed, we both missed California and our friends, so we decided to go out for a visit. We arrived on a Wednesday in August 2012. Boy, were we happy! We had lunch with our very good friends, stayed at Gloria's, our god mom's house, and visited our church family that evening. It was amazing. We felt like everyone missed us as much as we had missed them. There were hugs and kisses all around. We planned on spending the whole trip with friends.

The next morning, we went for the walk we usually took when we had lived there. We had so much fun looking around the neighborhood to see what had changed. When we got home, we were still excited at what the day would offer. Then tragedy struck. Renda, my sister, called and we were having a regular conversation. My mom beeped in. When Renda clicked back to me, she was crying, and told me Asa, our younger brother had been found dead at home. I shouted, "Asa! Asa! But how? What happened?" I thought it couldn't be true. I had just spoken to him on Monday and he was fine. The last words my brother had said to me were , "I love you." The last words I said to my brother were, "I love you too. See you when I get back home."

My body went numb, and I could not stop crying. I told my sister I had to speak to our parents and check on them. Both of our parents have heart issues. I knew how much they loved each of us, and I became even more alarmed. I called and spoke to my dad. He said they had sent Asa, Jr. to check on his dad after Asa did not show up for work or answer the phone.

When Asa, Jr. got in the house and saw his dad, he knew right away that he was dead. My dad said he had to go. He and my mom needed to take care of the children and my sisters because everyone's heart was broken. With his voice filled with tears, my dad asked me if I was going to be okay. Wanting to protect him, I told him yes, but I think he knew differently. He asked to speak to Isiah and told him to watch over me. Isiah promised and told him we would be on the next available flight home.

My heart was broken. I had not felt this type of pain before and did not know how to put it in a place of peace. I stopped crying long enough to call my oldest brother, Harry, and tell him what had happened. I told him I would give him a little time to compose himself. I would call him back within the hour to help him make plans to travel home. Isiah held me so tightly, trying to comfort me; but for the moment I felt alone in my sorrow. I wondered, "How can I go on without talking to my brother? How are my parents going to survive this? What about his children? They no longer have a father." I asked Isiah to pray with me, so I could ask God to help me make sense of my emotions. As I prayed, I explained to God that I knew none of us are promised today or tomorrow yet my heart was broken with sorrow. I prayed He could help me to put this tragedy into its proper place and to help me mourn with understanding.

Isiah called our friends, Michael and Vatrice, who picked us up from the airport. They told us to come right over, and they would help us make all the arrangements to get home. They told us not to worry about anything. They would call all of our friends and let them know we needed to get back home immediately. This helped a great deal, but through my tears, I still could not wrap my mind around what was happening.

We made the arrangements to fly home later in the evening. Our friends came over, brought food, and encouraged me to eat, but I had no appetite. I was happy to see their love. It gave me peace to know that people really cared about us.

I called our three children and told them of the tragedy of Asa. They all cried, but Syrell mourned the most. He had had a special bond, one from birth, with his uncle. Asa had been a big part of his life when Syrell was growing up. We had lived in the same house. Asa spent long hours with my son, helping to mold him into a young man.

I called Syrell's dad. He and his wife, Terrie, helped make the arrangements for Syrell to fly home. We caught our flight and got home the next afternoon. We repacked our clothes and went straight to our parents' home. The house was sad, but Dad and Mom were trying to hold everything together.

My brother was married but had been separated from Mil, his wife of about 16 years. Mil was a great sister. Our family loved her deeply. She and my brother did family things together, but they couldn't live together. My parents loved her and decided that because Asa and Mil were still legally married, she had the authority to decide on the arrangements that had to be made. She decided family and friends would need to come to my parents' home. The funeral would also be at my parents' church. We all went to the funeral home and made plans together for the service. There was so much love and sadness in the room. Somehow, we all got through it.

The only thing I felt like I needed to start the grieving process, to accept the fact that I would never see my brother alive again, was to see his body. My heart would not accept that he was dead until I could see him. I spoke with my sister, and she said that she felt the same way. We went to the funeral home director and requested to see our brother. He told us the body had not arrived from the coroner's office. We could come and say our good-byes after they had seen to the condition of his body. My brother had died in his sleep. He had been home almost an entire day before he was found. The heat of the summer had sorely affected his remains. We still didn't understand the depth of the problem until a call came from the funeral home. We might need to consider a closed casket.

My sister and I were told to come to the funeral home at 5:00PM the next day. When we got there, we were told that we needed to see the director. He said we could not see Asa. They were trying to do everything in their power to make him presentable but it was a hard case. We told him we could not leave. We had to see him. The condition of his body did not matter. We just needed to make sure it was our brother. He understood and told us the only comfort he could offer was a few pictures for us to view. We could see them only if we promised not to show them to family members. We agreed. When he brought out the pictures, our hearts dropped. Even more pain was added to our broken hearts when we realized it was almost impossible to see Asa in the lifeless body on the photo. My sister and I looked more closely. We did recognize a mark on his face and knew we knew our brother would not breathe, laugh, joke, or play with us anymore. His eternity was sealed. All we had were our memories.

The next few days passed. The family made preparations to lay Asa to rest. The funeral home wanted to know if we wanted them to take the body straight to the church or bring it to the house and drive it to the church with the family. My dad made the call. He said, through tears, that Asa's body needed to be brought home. It would be his last visit home. Dad needed him to come by one last time, just one last time.

On the day of the funeral, James, his dad, and his brothers came over. They said there was no way they could not have come to pay their last respects to a man who always had nothing but kind things to say. They also said that we were family and always would be. I could tell how much this comforted Syrell. I was grateful for their thoughtfulness.

The funeral was on a weekday, so we thought the church

would be filled with only the closest of friends and family. When the funeral car pulled around the corner to the church, we were amazed to see the parking lot full. In fact, there were so many people, the overflow rooms were filled. At the funeral, we laughed and we cried, but most of all, we said good-bye to a wonderful and giving man.

A few days after the funeral, my parents called a meeting of the family. They wanted us to talk about how we were feeling. We needed to discuss the thoughts going through our heads and hearts. We talked and cried. We talked and laughed. Most importantly, we talked.

Thirteen

Taking Life One Day at a Time

How does one put the pieces back to their life when it has been torn apart? Do I just go on as if I hadn't lost a close loved one? How do I survive the loss of a person who had been part of my life for 45 years?

After the funeral, I started feeling like I was having some type of heart attack. My chest would hurt. I felt a need to go to the hospital; but instead, I would pray. This happened for weeks before I talked to my sisters about it.

They told me they had the same feelings. We concluded it was because we were suffering from broken hearts. Thank goodness for communication. I do not know where I would be today had it not been for our family talking through our true feelings.

I was happy to know that what was happening to me was normal. I also found myself crying every day for weeks. I would think of my brother from the moment that I awoke in the morning to the time I went to sleep at night. I mourned so much it felt like it was consuming my every moment.

One evening we were watching a movie, called "Courageous," in which a tragedy had occurred. A dad had lost his daughter to a drunk driver. He had trouble getting his arms around it and went to his pastor for help. His pastor told him that when tragedies occur, we all have two options. We can blame God for the time we did not have with our loved one, or we could be thankful to God for the time we did have. A light went off; I now knew how to pray a more complete prayer for my grief.

I started thanking God for all the wonderful times we had had with our brother. I thanked Him for all the people who had come up to us at the funeral to tell us how much our brother had helped them. I thanked God for showing me how to mourn for and with others when they faced tragedy. I thanked God for putting in my heart the knowledge that one day in the future I would be able to see my brother in a place where we would be able to laugh together.

Through all of this, Isiah has been my rock. He hugged me when I needed a hug. He kissed me when I needed a kiss. He cried with me when I needed to cry. Most importantly, he was there!

Death has a way of making you look over your life. Who were you in your youth? How did you handle your teenage years? What kind of adult did you become? Would you change anything? How would you change it?

I thought about that little scared girl of Chapter One — how she lost her worth in one minute of time. I thought about how her abuse took a toll on not just her life but, also, on most of the lives around her.

Frequently I asked myself, "Why did Devil Man hurt me? Was he an object of abuse himself? Did he see something inappropriate happen to his mom that peaked his sexual interest?" Any of these things could have happened, but the bottom line is that he made a choice. His choice was to hurt and destroy.

Forgiving him with all of my heart was the part I had to train myself to do. The Bible says that we should love our neighbor as ourselves. This can be hard because a lot of us forget to love ourselves. If you've been hurt, it can be even harder to like yourself, let alone love yourself. It is achievable, however, through the Word of God. Once I saw that God had mercy on me and cast my sins as far as the East is from the West, I did something children do; I believed it. I believed I was forgiven.

After I looked at my own life and saw how many people I had hurt, I found it easier to forgive a man who had been walking in the darkness. I forgave Devil Man much because I had been forgiven much.

That little girl had no strength; but today, I tell anyone who will listen about my life. I want others to know they are not alone in their pain. I will be your voice until you have a voice of your own!

Fourteen

Until we Meet Again

Would Anyone Cry for Me? I now believe someone would. The biggest reason is that I will now cry for anyone.

If this book has encouraged you in any way, Please be a part of our Movement to be a Voice for Hurting Hearts. This book will stretch around the world with your help.

Encourage everyone you know to support our "Would Anyone Cry For Me?" Movement and purchase their copy of Would Anyone Cry For Me?

I Love You All, Betty

Would Anyone Cry For Me?

ABOUT THE AUTHOR

Betty Thompson Haygood

In 2011 Betty decided to put her life on paper in order to help a hurting world. She finally understood that by telling her story she would help the millions of abuse victims who needed to find their own voice.

Betty believes that healing starts with one voice at a time. She decided that she would be that voice until each of you has a voice of your own. Her story ends with happiness, hope, and love. First she found love for herself and now she is able to share her love with others.

Betty Thompson-Haygood is a native of Hopkins, SC. She currently lives in Fountain Inn, SC, with her husband, Isiah. She is the proud mother of three: Taiasha Haygood, Vent Syrell (Angela) Abercrombie Jr., and Shameka (Joshua) Porter.

She has two wonderful grandchildren, Trevante and Julian Abercrombie.

Would Anyone Cry For Me?

To Schedule a Speaking engagement call: 864.404.9030

Our mailing Address is: P.O. Box 80691, Simpsonville, SC 29680.

WWW.WOULDANYONECRYFORME.COM

Would Anyone Cry For Me?

To order additional books or see specials visit our website:

WWW.WOULDANYONECRYFORME.COM

or call us:

864.404.9030

Would Anyone Cry For Me?

CPSIA information can be obtained at www.ICGtesting.com
Printed in the USA
LVOW040034100912

298071LV00001B/6/P